A
Journey
Of
Miracles

PHYLISS J. ESPOSITO

Contents

PART 1: MY STORY

PART 2: PRAYER AND VISUALIZATION

Acknowledgments

To My Family...
To my Suzanne, whose little hand held me up.
To my Jennifer, whose strength gave me courage.
To Jeffrey, who tried to make sense of it all.
To my Lauren, who is always there for me.
To my Ryan, who makes me laugh.
To Robert, for letting me be me.

Most of all,
to my God, who made it all possible...

❊ ❊ ❊

A Special Thank You
to
Father Mendez, and Father Evans, for their
Faith and Encouragement.
Derek Murphy for the cover & Keidi Keating for editing..

Introduction

IN AN INSTANT, I was transformed. Transported beyond time and space into the loving arms of God.

The day started out like any other day, yet it wasn't. While each day is a masterpiece unto itself, this day was especially beautiful.

It was spring, and nature was showing off in all its glory. The baby blue sky made a perfect backdrop for the pink and white blossoming trees that swayed back and forth in the warm spring breeze. I remember hearing church bells ringing in the background as I placed my order and chatted with my favorite coffee barista.

The splendor of that magnificent day made me think of God. I had been ignoring Him lately and Easter Sunday was fast approaching, so I decided to attend Mass.

As I entered through the massive wooden doors of the church, I could hear the ceremony already in progress. I tip-toed in just in time to receive Holy Communion. I hadn't been to confession in months, maybe years. As I stood in line to receive Him, it happened...

❋ ❋ ❋

...like a bolt of lightning, in a split second, I was suddenly and instantly surrounded by His love. I felt suspended in time. I felt His presence. I was engulfed in His love, bathed in His tenderness and mercy. There was no condemnation, only unconditional love. And in that moment I knew.

I was in a state of grave sin that day when I approached the altar to receive Him. I felt it was no one's business what I did or didn't do. If I wanted to receive Jesus in Holy Communion, I was going to receive Him, sin or no sin. But I was wrong. I knew it the minute I felt His touch. It was as though He was teaching me through His love.

It's hard to put into words the overwhelming feeling I felt that day in the presence of God. It was something so out of the realm of reality that it's almost impossible to explain. Nevertheless, it happened.

His love changed me. How can you disrespect Someone who loves you that much? Now I find it impossible to receive Him without confessing even the tiniest sin. He deserves the best, not second best.

I didn't know then that what had happened to me on that beautiful spring morning was part of a Divine plan. A plan that left me feeling puzzled and confused. A plan that thrust me in a direction I never intended to go.

God has always been an important part of my life, but for some reason, I put Him on the back burner. I lost my way. I was too busy living life on my terms to be bothered with His. How could I do that to Someone who had always been there for me?

Since my earliest recollection, I've had a connection with Jesus; nothing quite as profound as feeling His presence, but certainly experiences that defy all logic and reasoning. That's why I'm writing this book, to share these experiences with you. I hope in reading this book, it will give you hope when there is none, and something to cling to when you can't see a way out.

There is a God. He is REAL and He is always with you. He is a loving, caring Father who only wishes to love you. His love is open to all who seek Him, even sinners like me.

This book is about my journey. It's a journey of miracles, spontaneous healing, intuitive feelings, and messages. It's about the supernatural power of faith.

My deepest desire is for you to know Jesus, as I do: as a loving Father who cares for the little guy, the discouraged, the suffering, and the sinner. You don't have to be holy to approach Him. He is happy to meet you right where you are. You just have to believe and open your heart long enough to listen to His calling.

God still heals. He still performs miracles. Remember, He chose simple fishermen to be His disciples. All of them were flawed, and dysfunctional in their ways, yet He turned them into saints. Once you've experienced God's love, you can never go back. His love is all encompassing. You will find yourself on a quest for more. To learn more, do more, be more, your prayer time will become more meaningful, and suddenly, your self-centered nature will put others first.

Growing up Catholic, I thought I knew everything there was to know about God. Wrong! On my journey, I've uncovered many hidden gems which I'm excited to pass on-to you. It's mind boggling the signs and wonders Jesus left for us as a pathway to Him and His mother.

My journey back in time is one of exploration, frustration, and exhilaration. It's about a little girl's prayer. A young woman's struggle. And most of all, it's about God's saving grace.

This book is not about me. It's about you. I pray that while flipping through its pages, you discover your path and your purpose. I hope you find, hidden between the lines, encouragement, faith, and hope, folded gently into words, and a sprinkle of laughter to lighten your day. And most of all, I hope you find His Divine presence.

PART 1

My Story

1

My First Encounter

WITH TEARS STREAMING down my face and my nose pressed against the bedroom window of our tiny second-floor apartment in Brooklyn, I watched my mother run across the street in the pouring rain to catch her bus for work. She waved at me as usual, checking to see if I was all right. I wiped my tears away, and waved back. This was our Monday through Friday ritual. I'd come home from school at 3 p.m. and she would leave for work at 3:15 p.m. She worked the four-to-midnight shift as a candy packer for a local supermarket. I must have been seven or eight years old at the time.

I felt sadder than usual that rainy afternoon. Maybe it was because I hadn't had the chance to tell my mother about the A-grade I received on my religion test. A-grades were unusual for me, as generally I was a B-student.

I felt scared and alone even though I knew my brother Michael would be home from school soon. He was seven years my senior and was in high school. While I waited for him to come home, I sat in the bedroom chair next to the window while Baby, my cat, rubbed up against my legs. Somehow Baby always knew when I felt upset. He would jump on my lap in an attempt to comfort me as I cried my eyes out.

Months before, I had bought my mother a plaque with a picture of Jesus on it for her birthday. I took it out of the dresser drawer and held on to it for dear life, with Baby in my lap and tears running down my cheeks, I talked to the picture.

"God, please make my mommy stay home with me. Please make her stop working. Please God, please!" I kept repeating those words over and over again, kissing the picture at the same time, which only added to the drama. I was having my own private pity party when I heard Michael's key turn in the door.

The next morning, I awoke to the aroma of pancakes. I could hear my mother whistling which was my call to get up for breakfast. She whistled this funny tune to let me know it was time to get ready for school. As I watched her flip the pancakes, she seemed to be in an unusually good mood. As she put the plate on the table, she said, "I have a surprise for you."

"Is it Saturday I asked?" "No," she replied. "Last night for some strange reason I decided to change my shift at work. That means I'll work when you're in school and be here when you get home." I jumped out of my seat and hugged her so tight my arms hurt. I ran to the bedroom, picked up the picture of Jesus, and gave Him a big fat kiss. "Thank you, God! Thank you!"

I never thought what had happened to me that rainy afternoon was a miracle. I was a child. What did I know? I just expected God to answer my prayer and He did.

As an adult, I came to realize that this was the first of many miracles I would encounter, including spontaneous healing. It was the beginning of a lifelong friendship and incredible journey with a loving and merciful Father.

It isn't because I'm special or holy or any of those things. In fact, it's precisely because I'm the opposite.

One day, I was in this little Adoration Chapel that I go to, (I'll tell you more about that later.) I had just received an answer to a prayer, not the one I expected but one that would change my life forever.

It was something so out of the realm of my thinking that to this day I'm puzzled. As I sat there, I asked God, "Why me Lord?" I picked up the Bible and started randomly flipping through the pages. What was I thinking? That God was going to stop me on the right page, or an angel was coming down from Heaven, to hand me a note? God is a God of many surprises, and this is the page I landed on:

CORINTHIANS 1:27
But God hath chosen the foolish things of the world to confound the wise, and God hath chosen the weak things of the world to confound the things which are mighty;

****** Food For Thought ******

Learn to spot the miracles in your life. We all have them. Getting up each morning is a miracle for example. Finding a parking space after praying for one is another. Sometimes it's as simple as getting a good night's sleep, or witnessing a magnificent sunset that takes your breath away. Miracles come in all shapes and sizes. You simply have to notice them.

2

Summer with Grandma

EVERY SUMMER FROM the age of nine, until my mother realized I was old enough to stay alone while she worked, I would pack my suitcase and go with my Italian grandmother to Springfield, Massachusetts to spend the summer with Aunt Vinnie and Uncle Flori.

I hated going to Springfield. My grandmother was very strict, while I was very mischievous, which was not a good match. I was mesmerized as I watched Uncle Flori pull up to the train station in his big black shiny Cadillac to collect us. Uncle Flori was from my grandfather's side of the family, (the rich side), and the only side Grandma spoke to. As the car turned into the circular driveway towards this great big beautiful house, I thought to myself, 'someday I'll have a house just like that.'

When Uncle Flori opened the huge double glass entrance doors, I felt like I had stepped into Heaven. Everything in the house was white. The carpet was white, the furniture was white, even the cat was white. I remember I had to take off my shoes and tip-toe across the large living room to get to the door leading to the basement. For some strange reason everyone wanted to go there. I could never figure out why. The basement was ugly and was nothing like the Heaven upstairs. It was one large room which consisted of a kitchen and a den. It had dark brown paneling on the walls and two tiny windows. Yet, it was the gathering place for the entire family. A place to relax and wear shoes. It was where everyone shared Sunday dinner, which usually consisted of never less than ten.

Grandma and I shared a bedroom off to the side. It was a pretty room with its own bathroom, which was a plus, but I was still miserable. I wanted to be at home with my friends, rather than sleeping with Grandma who snored so loud she could blow the roof off.

Springfield was not my idea of fun. Don't get me wrong; I loved my grandmother. She was the only one to step up to the plate and watch me for the summer which took the pressure off my mother who had to work. One night when Grandma was sleeping, I snuck upstairs to investigate Heaven. To my amazement, it turned out to be a plastic Heaven. The entire upstairs was covered in plastic. There were plastic slipcovers on the sofa, the chairs, and even the dinning room table was covered in a plastic tablecloth. I'm surprised they didn't cover the cat in plastic too. The next thing I knew, Grandma was pulling my hair. "What are you doing up here? Get downstairs before I break your head." She mumbled something in Italian and pulled me by the ear down to the dungeon. That night, I slept on the floor out of spite.

I was always in trouble, but at the age of nine, I was bored out of my head and looking to go home. One day, my grandmother decided to make ravioli. She always made everything from scratch. During a punishment for chasing the cat, I sat there and watched her gently roll the dough. Then she cut it into little squares before placing a spoonful of ricotta cheese on top, and then she added another square on top of that, until it looked like a mini ricotta sandwich. As I watched her pinch the edges to seal the ravioli, my mouth watered. After she finished tweaking the ravioli, she lovingly placed each one on a white cloth on the kitchen table. When she finished, she stood back and admired her work. "Finito! Perfetto!" That's when it hit me! Maybe this was my golden opportunity to get a reprieve? She was in a good mood and I was determined to take advantage of it. I ran up and gave her a fat kiss on the cheek. I flattered her with compliments about what a great cook she was, but she just patted me on the head and pointed to the chair. That was it! I was doomed. I figured if she punished me for doing something silly like chasing the cat, I might as well do something terrible to deserve it, so, when she wasn't looking, I put my thumb print on every single one of her perfect raviolis.

After the ravioli incident, I was banished to my room for the rest of the summer. One Sunday my cousin Ella stopped by for coffee. After hearing the famous ravioli story and laughing her head off, she offered to take me to her house. I guess she felt sorry for me. She told my grandmother she needed help with the baby. Ella had two sons David 13, and Ronnie 15, from a previous marriage. Pauli was the baby. He was three years old and a brat, just what I needed. Her sons were both in summer school, and she wanted help with Pauli while she worked.

Ella worked from home as a hairdresser. I figured being there was better than being with Grandma. Besides, I liked Ella, which is more I can say for the rest of the family. All they did was talk about her. I guess they were jealous. Ella was young, beautiful, and blonde. She drove a flashy blue convertible and she looked like Marilyn Monroe. I heard them say, they thought she was taking advantage of my cousin Jimmy because he had money and owned a successful bar. I believe it was just because Ella was different. She was fun, and I loved being with her. In fact, I wanted to be her. That's why, at the age of eighteen, I bought a convertible car and dyed my hair blonde.

Ella was young and free. There were no rules in her house. No bedtime either, just Pauli the brat. I used to take care of him when Ella's hair appointments arrived. If she had to pick up supplies at the store, she would leave me alone with him. Pauli was a terror. I have a feeling that was God's way of getting even with me for what I did to my grandmother. All Pauli did is cry and throw things. One day, he hit me in the eye with a baseball, and I had a shiner for over a week. Maybe Grandma wasn't so bad after all.

When my cousin Jimmy took the baby on weekends to visit family, Ella and I would hang out and go shopping in the convertible with the top down. I guess because she had three boys she liked being with a little girl. I watched her try on high heels, a nice change from the orthopedic shoes Grandma wore. She would buy me summer shorts, and lots of cute girly things. She waved my hair and put nail polish on my toes. She knew how to do everything. She even knew how to sew.

One day, during one of our excursions, Ella asked me to pick out a dress pattern from this great big book in the store. It was so much fun trying to choose a fabric from the hundreds of bolts leaning against the wall. I chose a black and white check fabric. Ella said she was going to help me make a dress so I could wear it home and surprise my mother. I found out later it was my mom who had called Ella and asked her to let me stay with her. Ella and Mom were good friends, and I guessed Mom sensed I was miserable with Grandma. That's why Ella stopped by that afternoon, it wasn't for coffee. It was for me.

After the baby was asleep my cousin Jimmy would teach me how to ride a bike. It was so freeing riding up and down the block, which is something I could never do in Brooklyn. Besides, I didn't have a bicycle. My mother thought it was too dangerous, and we couldn't afford it anyway. I learned a lot that summer, and everything was perfect. I was having the best time ever. Then one evening everything changed.

David and Ronnie were great to me at first. We would ride bikes, go hiking, and play cards. I felt like their little sister. One afternoon, they decided to climb a steep mountain with no path. I did okay going up, but when it came time to go down, I froze and started to cry, so David had to take me by the hand and lead me down. They never stopped teasing me about crying, and so I never cried in front of them again. We were so close that when Ella and Jimmy went out for the evening and left us alone to baby sit, I felt safe. I should have known better.

After Pauli was asleep the three of us would watch television together. One night David announced he was bored and wanted to do something different. I suggested we play a game of checkers. Ronnie suggested spin the bottle. I've played spin the bottle before, but we were usually a bunch of kids turning an empty soda bottle and kissing the one it pointed at when it stopped. My cousins said if the bottle landed on them they would just smack each other. I soon found out that David and Ronnie were not kids. They were teenage boys with more on their minds than kissing.

I was nine, pretty, and inquisitive. A dangerous combination. It all seemed like fun at first. We would laugh, eat candy, and goof around.

I started to feel uncomfortable when the kissing became more intense and lasted longer. First David would kiss me, and then Ronnie. I felt things were getting out of hand. When I tried to stop the game, they protested and made fun of me. Inside my head, I heard alarm bells going off. Something was wrong. I tried to get away, but they wouldn't let me go. I panicked, and under my breath, I cried out to God. "Help me, please. I'm afraid. Please get me out of here!" Before I could finish the sentence, I heard my cousin Jimmy call out, "Where is everybody?" I had never ran out of a room so fast.

After that, I lived in fear. I felt trapped. I was afraid to tell my cousin Ella, and I knew if I told Jimmy he would punish my cousins for life. So I kept quiet. Ronnie and David would tease me, hinting that they would get me next time we were alone. I was petrified, and I did everything I could to avoid them. When Ella and Jimmy went out, I would stay outside on the porch until they came home. I rode my bike until my legs hurt. One night while I was riding, it started to pour down. I had no choice but to go inside. I picked up Pauli and held on to him for dear life. I knew they wouldn't come near me with the baby in my arms. Pauli the brat, saved my life.

I wanted to tell my mother, but I didn't want to scare her, and I didn't think my grandmother would believe me. So, I continued to say nothing.

I hardly slept after that. I was afraid that David or Ronnie would sneak into my room in the middle of the night. I even pretended to be sick so that Ella would stay home. I hugged my pillow at night and prayed. "God please get me out of here. Please let my grandmother come and take me. I want to go home. Please God, please!" I would cry myself to sleep almost every night.

The following morning I heard a familiar sound. It was the horn on my father's truck. I ran to the window as his big yellow tractor trailer pulled up to the house. All the neighbors came out to see what was going on. They thought my cousins were moving. When God sends help, He does it in a big way.

My father was a truck driver for ABC Trucking. He hauled merchandise cross-country. I hardly ever saw him. I remember when he was home, he would pick me up at Saint Agatha's School in the truck and we would have lunch together. Those were great times. I adored my father even through; I never saw much of him. I became Miss Popularity with the boys at school because of that truck. They all wanted a ride in it.

I ran to my father and hugged him so tight. He had no idea how happy I was to see him. He bent down and picked me up. Ella ran out to greet him. "What are you doing here?" she asked. "I was passing and wanted to stop by and see my girl." Ella told my father about all the fun we were having and how I was such a big help. I stood there frozen with fear. "Please God let him take me home. Please!" I wouldn't dare tell my father what was going on, as he would have gone after the boys. Instead, I just prayed. Then I heard those magic words: "Since I'm here, I might as well take my daughter home with me. Summer's almost over, and I'll be home until she goes back to school." My heart nearly jumped out of my chest. "Thank you, God! Thank you!"

I had packed my suitcase after the first kissing session, so I was ready. I ran inside, picked up my suitcase and kissed Ella goodbye. I thanked her for everything and grabbed onto my father's arm. Ella came running out of the house as my dad was lifting me into the truck. "Wait! You forgot to take the dress you made." I never returned to Springfield again.

***** Food For Thought *****

Teach your children to speak out if something is wrong.

Today kids are much smarter than I was, but, with the invention of the Internet, they are more likely to put themselves in danger.

If You Are A Kid

Be aware of any activity that doesn't seem right, or if someone insists on friending you on Facebook or any of the other social media sites. If anyone seems strange or starts getting too personal, keep away. If you are bullied, made fun of, or abused, in any way, shape, or form, it's wrong and unacceptable. Be careful of pictures and selfies you post. Remember, the Internet never forgets. If you feel uncomfortable about anything, or anyone, then SPEAK OUT! TELL SOMEONE. It could save your life.

3

Unbelievable Findings

AS A CHILD growing up in a Catholic school, I learned lots of things, but most of all I learned all about fear. It seemed everything was about sin, punishment, and Hell. As a young impressionable kid who hated rules, I couldn't figure out why the God that was always there for me was so darn strict. I thought we had a perfect relationship. I asked, He gave. Why mess up such a good thing with all those rules?

It seemed everything I did was a sin. I couldn't eat meat on Friday; I couldn't do this; couldn't do that, and besides the couldn'ts, I had to go to Mass on Sunday. If I missed it, I committed a mortal sin, and I was going to Hell! Unless of course, I went to Confession where everything was forgiven. I thought that was a pretty good deal. I could sin all I wanted, go to Confession on Saturday, and I'd be good to go for another week!

One week I missed Confession. I was so frightened that I was going to Hell, I refused to leave the house. Sister Angelica came to see me. She explained that God would never do anything like that to me. She taught me that Jesus gave us rules to protect us, not to punish us. And to teach us how to live and be happy. She taught me that God was love and mercy. That's why He gave us Confession. I clung to the love and mercy part because damnation was always looming on my horizon.

Even though I learned about God, I never really had a relationship with Him. That came much later. I only knew that every time I called on Him, He was there. I became more and more curious about Jesus as I grew up. I also felt guilty because I hated going to Mass. It was boring. I wanted to sleep on Sunday, not go to church. I couldn't figure out why it was such a big deal. So I asked the Sister. She explained that the white wafer I received at Mass was the Body and Blood of Jesus, and then she opened the Bible to read me a passage.

Matthew 26:26
As they were eating, Jesus took some bread and blessed it. Then he broke it in pieces and gave it to the disciples, saying, "Take this and eat it, for this is my body."

Sister told me that during the Consecration, the priest, through the power of the Holy Spirit, changes the bread and wine into the Body and Blood of Christ, in the same way Jesus did at the Last Supper.

"Why would Jesus want us to eat His body?" I asked. I must have had a disgusting look on my face because she smiled and said, "He wanted to give Himself to us so we could have eternal life with Him in Heaven." Then she read another passage.

John 6:52-54
Then Jews began to argue with one another, saying "How can this man give us His flesh to eat?" So Jesus said to them, "Truly, truly, I say to you, unless you eat the flesh of the Son of Man and drink His blood, you have no life in yourselves. He who eats My flesh and drinks My blood has eternal life, and I will raise him up on the last day."

Wow! How could you go wrong? You received Jesus in Holy Communion, and in return, He gives you eternal life. I suddenly realized why Mass was so important. Sister told me about the many Miracles of the Eucharist. "What kind of Miracles?" I asked. She told me that the first Miracle was in Lanciano, Italy and it dates back to the eighth century.

A Basilian monk, who had doubts about the real presence of Christ, was offering Mass when he pronounced the words of the Consecration, and the Host miraculously changed into live Flesh and the wine into live Blood. She said the miracle was visible to everyone in attendance.

"I don't believe it!" I shouted. She showed me pictures of the miracle. When I finally found my voice, I asked, "How do you know that the monk was telling the truth?" She said that over the years many scientific studies had been done to prove the authenticity of the Miracle. She said, "When you grow up, you can go to Italy and see the Miracle for yourself."

❈　❈　❈

Many years later, in 2010, I traveled to Italy to see the wonder for myself. My husband and I traveled via car from Rome to the quaint, Italian City of Lanciano, which is part of the Abruzzo region. It is so beautiful that it looks like a picture postcard with its little shops and cobblestone streets, and spectacular views of the countryside. We enjoyed seeing the beautiful Italian architecture and exploring the many lovely boutiques and coffee shops that lined its narrow streets. The most memorable moment was when we visited the Sanctuary of the Eucharistic Miracle, which takes residence in the Church of Saint Francis. We were awestruck. There, in a silver Ostensorium (holder) was the Flesh still intact, and the blood coagulated into five globules, irregular and differing in shape and size, yet all the same weight.

The Catholic Church officially claims the Miracle as authentic. It is visited by millions of people each year. Don't miss the opportunity to experience it for yourself.

Authentication & Information on the Miracle:

In 1970-71, and again in 1981:
Prof. Linoli and Prof. Bertelli did a scientific study.
The analyses conducted with absolute and unquestionable scientific precision. It was documented with a series of microscopic photographs. These analyses concluded the following:

The Flesh is real flesh.
The Blood is real blood.
Both are from a human species.
The Flesh consisted of muscular tissue of the "HEART."
Both Flesh and Blood were the same blood type: AB.

Note

The blood-type is identical to that which Prof. Bollone uncovered on the Shroud of Turin.

Shroud of Turin.

The Holy Shroud of Turin is believed to be the burial cloth of Jesus. The reddish brown stains show various wounds that according to proponents, correlate with the image of a crucifixion and the Biblical description of the death of Christ. Markings on the cloth have been interpreted as follows:

One wrist bears a large round wound, apparently from a piercing.
The second wrist, hidden by the folding of the hands has an upward gouge in the side.
There are small puncture wounds around the forehead and scalp.
There are scores of wounds on the torso and legs.
There is swelling of the face, and streams of blood down both arms.
The blood type on the Shroud is AB.

The Sudarium of Oviedo

The Sudarium of Oviedo is believed to be the cloth that covered the face of Jesus. The Blood type is also AB.

❉   ❉   ❉

In addition to being the rarest blood type: AB Plasma is universal and can be used for all patients regardless of their blood type.

More Miracles

At seven o'clock in the evening on August 18, 1996, Fr. Pezet was saying Mass when a woman came to tell him she had found a discarded host on a candle holder. Fr. Pezet put the Host in a container of water and placed it in the tabernacle. On Monday, August 26, upon opening the Tabernacle, he saw to his amazement that the Host had turned into a bloody substance. He contacted the Archbishop, Jorge Mario Bergoglio (who is now Pope Frances.) The Archbishop witnessed the miracle and ordered it be photographed and examined.

Authenticity

In 2008, Dr. Castañón, a former atheist, at the Faith and Science Conference in Buenos Aires, Argentina, gave evidence to the findings of the Miracle. He also arranged to have the lab reports from the Buenos Aires Miracle compared to the lab reports from the Lanciano Miracle. The experts making the comparison concluded that the two lab reports must have originated from the same person. They further reported that both samples revealed an "AB" positive blood type.

Note

The Vatican has approved an exhibition of photographs of the Eucharist miracles that occurred around the world.

For info: Go to:

Vatican International Exhibition of the Eucharist Miracles.

Most Notable Miracles:

Siena, Italy - August 17, 1730
Consecrated Hosts remain perfectly preserved for over 250 years. Rigorous scientific experiments have not been able to explain this phenomenon.

Amsterdam, Holland - 1345
Eucharist thrown into fire overnight miraculously is unscathed.

Blanot, France - March 31, 1331
The Eucharist falls out of a woman's mouth onto an altar rail cloth. The priest tries to recover the Host, but all that remains is a large spot of blood the same size and dimensions as the wafer.

Bolsena-Orvieto, Italy
Again, a priest has difficulties believing in the Real Presence, and blood begins seeping out of the Host upon consecration. Because of this miracle, Pope Urban IV commissioned the feast of Corpus Christi, which is still celebrated today.

****** Food For Thought ******

We are so blessed that Jesus left us a trail of evidence and signs so that we may see and believe.

John 20:29
Jesus said to Thomas, "Because you have seen Me, have you believed? Blessed are they *who did not see, and yet believed.*"

4

A Strange Sensation

IN THE SIXTH grade, the only thing on my mind were boys, clothes, gossip, and Confirmation. Coming from a large Italian family, I knew that receiving a Sacrament was a big deal. It also meant lots of presents, food, and family celebrations.

The last Sacrament I received was Holy Communion in the second grade. I remember making the rounds with my father (that's what he called it). It was his way of showing me off to my relatives and making sure they didn't forget me.

We would go to my grandmother's house where my Aunts and Uncles gathered for Sunday dinner. They all lived within a small radius of each other. The trick was to get to her house before my cousins, who were all around the same age, and making the rounds too. My father made sure we were the first to arrive.

The minute I walked in the door looking like a bride, in my white Communion dress and tiara headpiece, everyone made a fuss. They forced me to twirl around like a ballerina so they could admire my beautiful dress with the rose petal bodice, tie ribbon waist, and tulle bottom. It even had tiny sequins woven throughout, which made me sparkle. I looked like a snowflake in head to toe white, and felt like a princess. I made sure everyone took notice of my shoes and little white pocketbook, reminding them what I was there for. They oohed and awed as they stuffed my purse full of money and my mouth full of food.

My cousins would get so mad when they walked in and saw me standing there. It was a game. We would call each other up and make bets on who would get there first. We knew if we arrived late we would only get candy. Grandma would say "You come late, you get nothing." But then she would wrap a few candies in a dollar bill and hand it to the latecomers.

When no one was looking, we would sneak off and hide in the bathroom to count our money. My cousins would lie about how much they received, knowing I arrived first and received the most. Then we heard Grandma yell, "What are you kids doing in there?" We took off like jackrabbits and ran into the backyard to play ball. No one messed with Grandma.

They were great memories, believe me, my father gave more than I received. My family was poor in the pocket but rich in the heart.

Confirmation day couldn't come fast enough. I was so excited and full of anticipation it was hard to sleep. I would lie awake dreaming about what kind of outfit I would get, instead of concentrating on the Sacrament I was about to receive.

Sister Madeline, my religion teacher, taught us that Confirmation is one of the seven sacraments. The other six are Baptism, Confession, Holy Communion, Holy Orders, Matrimony, and Anointing of the Sick. Sister taught us when we receive Confirmation, the Holy Spirit descends upon us, just like He did to the disciples. Then she read us a passage from the Bible:

Matthew 28:19
Jesus said to them, "go therefore and make disciples of all nations, baptizing them in the name of the Father and of the Son and of the Holy Spirit."

Sister said the Spirit is the Advocate, the Helper. He infuses us with the Fruits of the Spirit which are: strengthen, wisdom, courage, and understanding, so we can proclaim the faith. He also imparts us with right judgment, reverence, and holy fear of the Lord, which means the desire not to offend God. Sister said it's the same as respecting our parents. She proceeded to tell us that the Holy Spirit is the third part of the Trinity (Father, Son, Spirit.) Three Persons in One God. I was shocked to hear that. I raised my hand and asked sister how God could be Three Persons?

Sister proceeded to tell the class that it's one of the greatest mysteries of the Catholic Church. She said that only a Divine Intelligence could conceive such a thing. She showed us a comparison by drawing a picture of an egg on the blackboard. She used it as an example to help us understand by looking at something visual. "Look at the egg and its three separate but equal parts: the yolk, the white, and the shell. Each has its own identity and purpose, yet all three make up something more. Take away one of the three parts, and it's no longer an egg."

As a child, I accepted without question. As an adult, I can now see the proof. In creation, I see the Father, in Jesus, I see salvation, and in the Spirit I learned the truth.

Confirmation day was fast approaching. We couldn't afford a party, but Mom made my Confirmation special nonetheless. Besides, she knew I'd be making the rounds with my father.

In Confirmation, you get to pick a sponsor; someone who takes on the responsibility of bringing you up in the faith if something should happen to your parents. We also got to choose a middle name. My Aunt Jo, Mom's sister, was my sponsor, so I took her name which is Josephine.

A week before the big day, my mother took me shopping. We perused the stores along Fifth Avenue where I lived in Brooklyn. After going in and out of every store, we finally settled on a beautiful periwinkle blue knit ensemble. It had a straight skirt, and the matching top had a mandarin collar, three-quarter sleeves, and a white embossed Oriental design on the front. Unfortunately, I had to hide it under the white gown with a red collar that was mandatory. I also had to wear a red skull cap. My shoes were the only thing I could show off. They were tan mid-high heels. I felt all grown-up as I walked down the aisle of the church to take my seat.

The bishop was coming to perform the ceremony, so everything had to be perfect. The church looked dazzling in red and white carnations, placed strategically around the altar and hung with a red ribbon on every pew. The church was small and limited in space so the sponsors couldn't attend; only the parents were allowed to come. The church chose a Deacon to represent the boys, and a Nun to stand up for the girls.

My aunt was so disappointed when she found out she couldn't attend the ceremony that she threatened to skip the collection basket next time at Mass. To console herself, she made a special dinner for me the night before the occasion.

I was full of enthusiasm as I walked with my mother and father down those few short blocks to my aunt's house on Fourth Avenue and Forty Third Street. I loved visiting my Aunt Jo and Uncle Nathan and hanging out with my cousins Joann and Natalie. We were a year apart, first Natalie, Joann, and then me. I have so many great childhood memories with them. My aunt promised she'd make me my favorite dinner, macaroni and meatballs! As we got closer to her house, I could smell the aroma of her spaghetti sauce as it permeated down the block and circled the entire neighborhood. After supper, the adults played cards, while my cousins and I played Monopoly. I was such a bad loser. If someone bought the Boardwalk before I had the chance to buy it, I'd throw the board in the air, and scream, "Game over!"

My father had to work the day of the ceremony, but he managed to stop by the church with his yellow truck. I kept turning around until I saw his face peek in the back door. After the ceremony, my best friend Marilyn and her mother joined Mom and I for lunch. Marilyn's mother worked, too. Her father left when she was a baby, so it was natural that we would become best friends.

I remember everything about Confirmation as though it were yesterday, but one thing in particular stands out. As we waited in line like soldiers ready to be deployed, I felt my hands start to sweat, and I was trembling. The thought of the bishop slapping me was upsetting. Sister assured us that it was part of the ceremony and only a tap. She said it was indoctrination into the Body of Christ and made us ready to proclaim the faith. I still felt scared. The bishop seemed overpowering, especially to a little kid of ten. He stood there in his elaborate red garments and head-piece which formed a point at the top, and I was so frightened as I approached him. The fear quickly dissipated as I drew closer, I noticed he had a kind and gentle face with a big smile. I relaxed. Then he softly tapped my cheek, made the sign of the cross in oil on my forehead, said some words as the sponsor held my shoulder, and it was over. I walked back to my seat and sat down feeling so relieved.

As I sat there, I contemplated the gifts I would receive when my father took me to make the rounds. Than I heard the bishop blessing us in the Spirit. Suddenly...

※　※　※

...I felt this strange sensation in the middle of my chest. It wasn't a pain, but more like a pressure. It felt like someone was pushing down on my chest with their hand. As quickly as it came, it went. I recall thinking, that's weird! I looked around to see if anyone else was holding their chest. But if they were I didn't see them. As I looked around I noticed that things appeared different and I couldn't figure out why. It was as though a light had been switched on inside me, and I was amazed to see how everything seemed brighter and bolder. The color red on the bishop was beaming, and the entire church seemed to sparkle. I felt happy, joyful, and filled with a sensation of peace. I starting praising Jesus under my breath, feeling an overwhelming love for Him. It's a feeling I'll never forget. For the first time in months my attention turned to Him. I made the sign of the cross and never said a word to anyone about it, until now.

Much later in my life, my cousin Natalie acknowledged that she went to a Healing Mass and had the craziest experience. She said that when the priest put his hand on her head and prayed for the Holy Spirit to heal her, she felt a strange pressure in the middle of her chest, like someone was pushing down on it.

****** Food For Thought ******

God loves us so much that He gave us the Bible (His Word,) so He can speak to us. He sent His only Son Jesus Christ who became man so we can relate and identify with Him and His sufferings. He gave us a visual of Himself on the cross to remind us how much He loves us. The Holy Eucharist (His Body and Blood) for nourishment and strength. The Holy Spirit to live within us to encourage and guide us on our journey. He even gave us His Mother as our Mother, when He died on the cross. A Mother to care, intervene, and provide a pathway to Him. The Saints to serve as inspiration of who we can become, and Guardian Angels to watch over us in times of trouble. He gave us the right to call Him Father with a simple prayer. And most importantly, He gave us free-will.

5

A Hand On My Shoulder

BROOKLYN WAS A great place to grow up, especially when I was young, single, and had a shiny new convertible. My friends and I would ride up and down Eighty-Six street, which at the time was the equivalent of South Beach, Miami. We were carefree as we drove down the avenue with the top down and the radio blasting. At the time, it was unusual for a girl to drive, let alone have a car of her own.

High school was finally over, thank God. I could never really cut it, and I quit before graduation. My mother was so upset. She tried everything to get me to go back to school. She even tried bribing me by offering me five hundred dollars towards college if I went back to get my diploma. I refused. She wanted to do the same for me that she had done for my brother. Michael took the money and went off to college, while Mom and I shopped for a new car. It was her way of getting me to take the money. She used it as a down payment on a midnight blue, Chevrolet Leman's convertible, with white bucket seats. She made the excuse that she was tired of taking the bus to work. In return I promised to pay the loan and drive her to work.

I know deep down inside Mom surmised I wasn't college material. It wasn't for lack of trying, as I later found out that I have a learning disability. Kids and adults with learning disabilities see, hear, and understand things differently. I learn by watching, listening, and doing. I have the strangest abilities...

For Example:

...I can't figure out fractions, yet, I could scale a room with a glance and come out with the same square footage as a contractor. One of the greatest gifts my mother ever gave me was something she used to say. "You can be anything you want if you put your mind to it." Those words became the mantra that carried me through the hard times. I never knew I couldn't, so I did. I gave myself the title of whatever I wanted to be and just did it.

My brother was smart, while I was social. He graduated college, enlisted in the army and then went on to become a Green Baret. I learned how to put on makeup and dance. Marilyn and I practiced dancing every day after school. If I wasn't with Marilyn, I was with my boyfriend, Charles. Charles was not only gorgeous, but he was also rich. He came from a gated community off the water near Coney Island called Seagate. At the time it was one of the wealthiest communities in Brooklyn. My friends envied me, especially when Charles came to pick me up in his red Corvette convertible. I was pretty, well-dressed, and had a great vocabulary, another surprising ability since I couldn't read well. I looked good and played the part, but inside I was hurting. I felt insecure, ugly, and stupid; a fact I hid from everyone. So, when I failed a test, I pretended it didn't matter. Charles was always my excuse. If it wasn't Charles, it was someone else. I used friends, popularity, and boys to validate me.

When you grow up the way I did, living in constant fear and insecurity, it changes you. My father, who I loved dearly, had a problem that became worse as I grew older. He liked to gamble, and when he gambled, he drank. I never knew what to expect when he was home. If he won, everything was fine. If he didn't, there was a royal battle. I was afraid of what I'd encounter when I arrived home, so I never had friends over. When I went on a date, I had the boy pick me up outside. My life was one big secret.

One day I came home to find my mother and father arguing and throwing things at each other. I was so afraid they would hurt one another that out of desperation, I ran upstairs to Mister Morrell, our neighbor. The Morrell family was my refuge. They were a big family with six kids. I was friends with Mary, their eldest daughter. Fights in my home were a constant occurrence. It seemed every other day when my father was around, I was running upstairs for help. I caught hell from my mother every time I did, as she was a very private person, and resented me telling anyone what was going on. She also resented me for loving my father so much and for looking just like him. I couldn't blame her, she had a tough life and suffered a great deal.

My parents tried. They certainly loved my brother and me, but sadly my father loved the horses more. My mother hated his gambling, and I can't say I blame her since we were always dodging bill collectors. After a while, my parents separated. I felt like the odd man out because I was the only one of my friends, except for Marilyn, who lived in a single-parent home. I think that's why I depended on God so much. He was always there for me. My faith pulled me through and gave me the courage to keep moving forward.

I can remember coming home from high school one afternoon and seeing the yellow truck parked in front of my apartment house. I ran upstairs thinking my father was moving back home. Instead, I found my mother reading the newspaper. I asked her, "Where's Dad?"

"In the kitchen," she said. I ran into the kitchen and found my father kneeling on the floor with his head in the oven. "Dad! What are you doing?" He answered with his head still on the oven door. "I'm gonna kill myself if she doesn't take me back." "Daddy please don't!" I ran inside to my mother. "Ma! Daddy has his head in the oven. He is going to kill himself if you don't take him back." She looked at me calmly and said, "Tell him to turn on the gas." That's when I knew it was over.

My mother and father finally divorced, and I moved in with my girlfriend, Susan. Marilyn had moved to Colorado by then. She wanted me to go with her, but I couldn't leave my parents. For some strange reason, I felt responsible for them, especially with my brother gone. My brother and I took care of our parents until they passed away.

❊   ❊   ❊

I had a job at Century 21, a clothing chain that sold high-end-fashion at discount prices. I wanted to be a model, so it was a perfect fit. I could pay for my car and save money on clothes at the same time. Susan was a beautician and used me as her model whenever she wanted to try a new color or hairstyle. That's how I became a blonde like my cousin Ella.

I was having the time of my life, partying, and staying out late. I never gave Mass or God a thought. I was too busy having fun. Until that one night...

❊   ❊   ❊

...that warm, intoxicating summer night. The top was down on the convertible, and Sue and I were singing to the blasting music. I felt strong, invincible, safe, as we sped down the parkway. It was Wednesday night, and we were on our way to the Mambo Lounge near Kennedy airport. Tito Puente was appearing there, which meant Latin dancing and hot guys. Like a bolt of lighting, an ominous, souped-up black convertible, with five creepy guys in it pulled up along side of us. I knew from the seductive smirk on the driver's face that we were in trouble. The guys in the back seat were either drunk or stoned and kept yelling obscene and vulgar remarks at us trying to get our attention. I attempted to stay calm, but Sue started fighting with them. The driver kept moving into my lane, trying to push me off the road. He shouted for me to pull over. I floored the car and took off. I was eighteen and an inexperienced driver, so I panicked.

My inner voice kept telling me to slow down, but as the gangbangers accelerated, I made a quick turn and cut across two lanes of traffic and lost them. I must have been doing 80 at the time. I heard horns honking and sirens going off. I knew the sirens were the police. I could see them in my rear view mirror, and I was glad to have them on my tail.

Suddenly, as I approached the end of the exit, I saw a stop sign. I immediately slammed on the brakes and lost control of the car. There were no seat-belt laws at the time, so we had nothing to protect us. I screamed out, "God help us please!" The car was spinning, and Sue was holding on for dear life. We were both screaming as the car started to slide in the ditch. All of a sudden, I felt someone grab my shoulder, protecting me from being thrown out of the car. I grabbed onto Sue as the car landed in the ditch.

I must have blacked out, because the next thing I know, a policeman was asking if I was alright. I looked over at Sue who seemed to be okay. I tried to move but realized the car was on its side. The paramedic said it was a miracle we weren't both killed, as he lifted me onto the stretcher and into the ambulance. I got a glimpse of the car as they towed it from the ditch, just before I closed my eyes.

Weeks later, after we had a chance to recover from the accident, Sue and I sat down to discuss what happened. I felt strange telling her my story, for fear she'd think I was making it up. To be honest, I wasn't sure myself if I had really experienced it. I decided to tell her anyway, so I blurted it out. "Remember when we were sliding into the ditch, well, I felt someone grab me by the shoulder." Sue looked at me like I had three heads. I knew it! She thought I was crazy, but to my amazement she said she felt the same thing. "How can that be?" She asked. "There was no one in the car but us, so who grabbed us, the invisible man?" "I have no idea, but I know I felt a hand on my shoulder. It had to be God!" She started to laugh. "Don't be ridiculous, there's got to be a logical explanation." "What? Someone was walking on the highway, saw us about to plunge into the ditch, and jumped in the back seat to save us?" She thought for a moment, then shouted out, "You're right! It had to be God! It had to be Him!"

As we both acknowledged the miraculous blessing we received, we broke out in tears. It allowed us for the first time to release the tension we felt. We went to Mass the next day, and gave thanks to the Lord for being alive, and for saving two stupid kids from a disaster, on that warm, intoxicating summer night.

Another Strange Occurrence

Several years later, another strange thing happened to me. I was driving to work one evening when out of the blue I felt this throbbing headache. I figured it was something I ate or didn't eat. By now, I had moved up to a managerial position at Century. I was working the evening shift, taking inventory. As soon as I got into work, I had a hot cup of tea and two aspirin, which made me feel slightly better. After a few hours, the headache came back with a vengeance. I was in so much pain that I couldn't think straight. I thought I must be coming down with something. My boss took one look at me and told me to go home.

It was dark and rainy when I left the store. I got into my car, took another aspirin, and started to drive home. I couldn't wait to get under the covers and go to sleep. As I pulled onto the highway, I began to feel light-headed. I felt like I was there, yet not there. I prayed for God to get me home safely.

As I drove, my head started to pound. It felt like someone was hitting me over the head with a sledge hammer. Then, just like that, I couldn't move my eyes. It was the scariest thing I've ever experienced. I mean, I really couldn't move my eyes. I couldn't look up or down. I literally had to raise my head to look up, and put my head down to look down, as though my eyeballs were frozen. My side vision was almost gone too. I was terrified, even writing about it now sends chills up my spine. I could feel my heart pounding. As the weather continued to worsen, it was impossible to see the road. I put my caution lights on and drove the rest of the way home like that. I swear to you, I have no idea how I got home.

As soon as I walked in the door, Sue took one look at me and drove me straight to the ER. I personally think I had a mini stroke, but back then, they didn't have MRI's, so there was no way of knowing what really happened. I checked out okay, and they sent me home. I never felt right after that episode. I continued to search out every doctor I could find, looking desperately for an answer to no avail. The results were always the same. Negative.

When you experience something so traumatic as I did, it doesn't just go away; it gets stored somewhere in your subconscious. It's like a

Cheetah waiting for its prey; you never know when it's going to pop out and attack you. I lived in constant fear that it would happen again. That one incident left such an indelible mark on me that to this day it still haunts me. It also led me on a journey I never intended to take, down a path of discovery and wonder, of extreme highs and terrible debilitating lows, a path of happiness and sadness, a path to God...

****** Food For Thought ******

Never let adversity stop you! You can do all things through Christ who strengthens you, so never forget that. Whether you are disabled, have a learning disability, come from a broken home, are uneducated or underprivileged, God has a plan for you. Have faith in Him, and faith in yourself, and never be afraid to cry out for help. It could save your life. Like it did mine.

6

❖

The Path

THE LABOR PAINS came long and hard. I was about to give birth to my first child. A girl. Our sweet little Suzanne.

Robert was handsome and he sang in a band. He played at a club in Brooklyn called Terry Lee's. He worked there to make money while going to college. I still had my job at Century 21 but dabbled in modeling, and not too long after, I was signed with Wilhelmina Modeling Agency in New York. To celebrate, Susan and I decided to go to Terry Lee's. We heard it was featuring a great new band called, THE YOU KNOW WHO'S.

From the moment Robert and I laid eyes on each other, we knew. I was eighteen at the time. He was twenty-one. During his break, he asked me to dance. The next thing I knew, we were an item. It was a perfect match. He wanted a career in music and I wanted one in modeling. Although everyone thought we were exclusive, we both saw other people. As soon as I felt someone was getting serious, I ran. I wanted nothing to do with marriage. After seeing what had gone on in my home, I vowed never to go down that road.

After Robert had graduated college, he decided to get a job in the music business. The band days were over, although I must say it was exciting traveling with him when he went on tour. He wrote a song called, MY LOVE ROSES ARE RED, and to his surprise, it took off. I joined him on many appearances. It was crazy to see the popularity of the band. The fans would wait outside to get his autograph. It was a scene trying to sneak away from the hundreds of screaming girls, all wanting to get their hands on Robert. It was fun, like a fairy tale, and then I became pregnant.

We were in love, so we decided to get married. We had no idea what we were getting into. We set up a home in a small apartment in Brooklyn not too far from our parents, and waited for our new arrival. Meanwhile, Robert pounded the pavement looking for steady employment.

Suzanne was the most beautiful baby I had ever seen. What did I know about being a mother? I was a kid myself. She brought such joy and happiness into our lives. She was so adorable, from the moment she held my finger, that day in the hospital when they placed her in my arms, I was in love, and a mom. She was our greatest joy. Robert couldn't take his eyes off of her. He would stand at the nursery window for hours just staring at her. In fact, we all stood there like statues staring at her, until the nurse finally rolled down the curtain blocking our view.

We were such fanatics that for the first few months we wouldn't let anyone touch her, and then eventually we gave in. She was the first grandchild on both sides, and we had to share. We were only kids, but she made us a family.

Robert landed a job with CBS Music. The only downside was that he had to travel to LA. It was the decade of sex, drugs, and rock & roll, and not easy on a new marriage. He made several trips a year to LA, sometimes I went with him, but it became increasingly difficult just to pick up and go. Robert stayed for weeks at a time, but at least he had a job. Everything seemed to be working out until he was asked to move there permanently.

It was a great opportunity so after thoughtful consideration, we decided that he should go and test the waters to see how he liked it. If all went well, we would join him. We didn't want to take the chance of uprooting our family until he was certain. We both understood that the music industry is a crazy, unpredictable business, and he could be out of work in a month. That's the way it was before CBS, he was always jumping from one record label to another. We lived paycheck to paycheck and hoped he still had a job at the end of the month.

The Holiday season was fast approaching, and Robert sent us tickets to join him in LA for Christmas. I promised Suzanne, we would visit Disneyland when we got there. She loved Mickey Mouse, but more importantly she needed to see her daddy. We said our goodbye's and I packed a bag and left.

Robert was happy at the job after living there for almost six months. He promised we'd look for an apartment as soon as I arrived. Unfortunately, it never happened. He was always too busy with his job, and every time I brought up the subject of moving, he avoided the question.

A part of Robert's job was to 'wine and dine' potential talent, which meant, after work dinners and late night meetings. Suzanne and I found ourselves alone most of the time. I felt sorry for my baby girl because she adored her father, and by the time he arrived home, she was fast asleep.

Robert knew I was unhappy being left alone. He invited me to parties when he could. I went to a few just to support him, but in the back of my mind, I was worried about Suzanne. I hated being apart from her, and I couldn't very well drag a little girl to a Black Tie event. Most of the time it was easier to just declined his invitation. I think he was relieved. This way he was free to fraternize the way he saw fit; besides, Suzanne and I were buddies. Let's face it, I was practically raising her by myself. I preferred to be with her, then go to some phony, pretentious, dinner party while they dished out drugs in the back room. I had enough of that nonsense with modeling.

The timing was wrong, and we both knew it. I left right after New Year's. We tried back and forth for another year, but on the way back from my last trip to LA, I decided to call it quits. I knew if I forced Robert to leave the job he loved, he would resent me. He deserved a chance to live out his dream, so I filed for a legal separation, as divorce was never an option as a Christian.

❆ ❆ ❆

We live our lives forward, but only truly understand it in retrospect. I know now that if I had gotten divorced, I would never have taken the path I'm on now, the path that was chosen for me.

❆ ❆ ❆

I was back home and struggling to make a living. I wasn't concerned about a path, church, God, or anything else for that matter. My only thought was to get a job and take care of my little girl. Robert sent me money, but it was barely enough to get by on, so as much as I hated leaving Suzanne, I had to work.

One of my dearest friends, Dottie, asked her brother-in-law Frank to give me a job at his trucking company. He offered me work answering phones and doing some paperwork. Dottie's mother Nancy watched Suzanne while I worked.

Dottie was a dear and wonderful friend until the day she died of lung cancer. She will be forever missed and forever in my heart.

I was getting my life together. I had saved enough money to move from the apartment I shared with Robert into a cute little one-bedroom walk-in, which was not only on the same block as Dottie, but two doors away. It made it easier for me to work, plus Suzanne would be starting pre-school soon, which was right across the street. I was enjoying life again, and even started dating. I was happy, content, or so I thought. Then one night, I heard a knock at the door...

❆ ❆ ❆

...It was Robert standing there with his suitcase. He had enough of Hollywood and wanted a second chance. Suzanne went crazy when she saw him. She loved her father, and it was hard for me to say no to her. So after a six-year separation, we reconciled. Eight months later I was pregnant.

The labor was much easier this time, even though Jennifer was a little chub weighing in at 10 pounds 4 ounces. We were overjoyed. Suzanne was seven at the time and waited patiently for her baby sister to arrive. She was so excited when the nurse placed Jennifer in her arms as we left the hospital. Suzanne watched over her sister like a lion looks after its cub. To this day Jennifer will go to Suzanne before she comes to me. They have a special bond.

Jennifer was a fun baby, mischievous like her mother. She was always climbing out of her crib. We would hear a loud thud and run into the bedroom to find her on the floor playing with her toys. She kept us jumping. She was the cutest little girl. She loved her food and still does. Life was good. Or so I thought...

※ ※ ※

...I knew something was wrong with me, but I couldn't put my finger on it. I was extremely exhausted all the time. I pushed myself, but that still small voice kept telling me something wasn't right. I went from doctor to doctor all telling me the same thing; it's stress, overwork, the baby. But I know my body and I knew they were wrong.

Robert was at another job, and I prayed this one would last. I never really trusted him after the breakup, even though he never gave me reason not to. I guess it was my own insecurity, I'm not sure. I protected myself by holding on to my friends, a job, and I kept a little money on the side just in case he decided to leave again. I felt safer that way. I swore to myself I would never be dependent on anyone again. I also didn't want my children to experience the abandonment I felt as a child and as a young mother.

I took over all the responsibilities of running a house and worked, too. I painted, decorated—you name it, I did it. Robert wasn't handy, so when it came to the big stuff, I called my father and cousin Augie. They always came to my rescue whenever I needed help.

I got the decorating bug from my mother. She loved fixing up our tiny apartment in Brooklyn and moving furniture around. I never knew where I would find the sofa when I came home. Her dream was to have a house of her own someday, but unfortunately, that day never came. I learned how to put up wallpaper and paint from my father. Every time he got into trouble from gambling, he painted the apartment to try and appease my mother. And guess who helped him?

I loved decorating, which I eventually turned into a business. I still dabbled in modeling a little thanks to my brother Michael, who worked at an advertising agency. He would get me work whenever he could. Wilhelmenia had to drop me because I didn't have the energy, or the desire to run into the city every time they called.

After being on my own for so long, I never wanted to be in a position to ask Robert for anything. I did whatever I could to earn money. Robert took care of the essential bills and food. I took care of everything else.

One day I received a call from my brother telling me to get to Virginia right away. His agency was looking to hire someone to do a national commercial. My mother took off from work to watch the girls while I ran off to Alexandria, Virginia to meet my brother. Michael picked me up at the train station. He told me the client was a good friend of his and not to blow it. I wasn't nervous until he said that. I had to make a good impression as I didn't want Michael to look like a jerk. Instead, I did exactly the opposite. My poor brother. I'm surprised I didn't get him fired.

Amtrack arrived late. We didn't have time to stop by his apartment so I could freshen up, instead, we went straight to his office. When we arrived, I ran into the ladies room to slip into my navy blue knit dress. It clung to my body giving me an hourglass figure and the dark color made me look thinner than normal. I put on my matching heels and fixed my hair and makeup. I looked professional. I straightened my dress and checked my lipstick in the mirror. I was in such a hurry, I didn't have time to give myself a complete once over. I just rushed out of the ladies room and down the hall towards my brother's office.

Michael was speaking on the phone when I opened the door and let myself in. He gave me the shush sign, so I tip-toed across the room and sat down. I checked my portfolio while I waited. This job was a big opportunity for me. A national commercial meant a lot of money. The first airing would be during a football game. The client was Van Heusen shirts. I was to be the fluff holding onto the sexy stud in the open shirt. Michael informed me as he hung up the phone that the client was on his way over. "Remember what I said, don't make me look bad." I wanted to kill him for reminding me. Now the pressure was on, and I could feel myself start to shake. My thoughts were interrupted by the knock at the door.

I quickly opened the zipper on my case, so I would be ready when he asked to see my portfolio. The knob turned, and in walked this handsome young man. I mean, drop dead gorgeous movie star looking man. I was so flustered, as I guess I had expected to see someone older. Michael stood up to introduce us.

"Phyliss, I'd like you to meet Nick. Nick this is my sister." As I got up to shake his hand, I tripped and knocked my portfolio on the floor. The headshots I had tucked into the side pocket of my case flew out and landed all over the floor. One picture landed right on the tip of Nick's shoe.

I could feel the blood rush to my head. I wanted to curl up into a ball and throw myself out the window. Michael picked up the pictures from the floor while extending his apologies to Nick. I just stood there shaking. Everything after that was a blur. Only the sound of Nick's laughter took me out of my catatonic state. I remember thinking, what a cool guy, he's laughing. Suddenly, I heard my brother's voice. "You okay kiddo?" That was Michael's nickname for me. He was shaking my shoulder. I just stood there completely frozen, not to embarrass myself any further.

Nick reached down and picked the photo off his shoe. He looked at the picture, then at me, and said, "How can I resist such a beautiful young lady who throws herself at my feet?" He smiled warmly and said, "You have the job." I uttered the words "thank you" and continued staring at him as he left the room. Michael started to laugh. "What's so funny?" I said. "Why didn't you tell me he was so damn good looking? I acted like a complete idiot. Thanks a lot!" Michael turned to me with a big smirk on his face, and said, "I didn't make you look like an idiot, you managed to do that all by yourself, now calm down before you give yourself a heart attack. Let's get something to eat, I'm starving."

My brother loved teasing me. As kids, we were always looking to get one up on each other. He definitely won this one. As I started to leave, he burst into laughter again. I turned back and gave him a look. "What now?"

"Wait!" he shouted. "Don't open that door! You have fingerprints all over your backside." "What?!" I looked, and sure enough, I had my fingerprints all over my navy blue dress. Then I remembered, I hadn't washed the makeup off my hands when I left the ladies room, some of it must have remained on my fingertips, so when I straightened my dress, I left my prints all over. "No wonder I was getting such strange looks as I walked down the corridor to my brother's office." Michael and I broke out in hysterics.

The commercial never aired. Right before it was set to go on, the game was interrupted with "Breaking News." I didn't become rich, but I did make a lasting memory with my beloved brother.

I worked hard to make sure Robert had as little stress as possible. He had enough of that trying to make a living and hold down a job. In the music business, you are only as good as your next hit. It was his job to find hit songs and place them with an artist. Now that we were home in New York, and had ample babysitters, I was expected to attend company functions. I was still feeling exhausted but pushed myself to go anyway.

Robert was moving up the ladder after landing a number one hit with the song MANDY, Barry Manilow's huge success. He had given the song to Barry via Clive Davis. We both felt a sigh of relief knowing that this meant security, at least for a little while. Robert was making enough money, so we were able to put a down payment on our first fixer-upper, and move out of my one-bedroom cramped apartment.

That one hit record changed our lives. Robert was in demand now. He was getting job offers every other day. Life was exciting. It involved travel, parties, the Grammy Awards, an expense account and all the pomp and circumstance that go with it. We were living high, then...

...I had my first attack...

❈ ❈ ❈

...It came like a thief in the night to steal my joy. It was during a Black Tie event. I felt detached. It's hard to explain, it was as though I was watching everything take place in slow motion. I felt dizzy, shaky, and disoriented. I went to the ladies room and splashed water on my face. I tried to compose myself but the room was spinning. I grabbed onto the sink. The next thing I remember, someone was helping me off the floor.

❋ ❋ ❋

Nervous breakdowns don't just happen. They creep up slowly like a Cheetah searching for its prey. I was about to be its prey.

****** Food For Thought ******

We are all under the illusion that we are in control. We plan our lives as though we are going to live forever. We work and study hard so we can make a decent living. We find a mate, have children, or a career. We buy a house if we're lucky, and work, work, work.

It seems everyone you meet today is busy. It's a full-time job just being busy. Then something happens: you lose a young friend, a parent, or your health, and suddenly you realize that you haven't spent enough time on what really matters.

Life is not ours for the keeping. It doesn't play by our rules. We are here for a purpose, to make a difference! To be kind to one another, to love, enjoy, and give thanks. Don't be foolish like the rich man that Jesus spoke about in the Bible...

Luke 12:13-21
"The ground of a certain rich man yielded an abundant harvest. He thought to himself, 'What shall I do? I have no place to store my crops.' Then He said... "This is what I'll do. I will tear down my barns and build bigger ones, and there I will store my surplus grain. And I'll say to myself, 'You have plenty of grain laid up for many years. Take life easy; eat, drink and be merry.'"

"But God said to him, 'You fool! This very night your life will be demanded from you. Then who will get what you have prepared for yourself?' This is how it will be with whoever stores up things for themselves but is not rich toward God."

Live in the moment! Your life can change in a split second. It happened to me. Just when I thought everything was fine, the bottom dropped out.

7

Anxiety and Panic

MY DOCTORS CONVINCED me that I had a nervous breakdown due to stress and overworking. They told me that what I had experienced that night at the party was probably an anxiety attack.

If you have never had an attack, you may not understand what I'm about to explain. Anxiety attacks are debilitating, paralyzing, and frightening events that seem to come out of nowhere. Your body goes into flight or fight mode and you feel like you're going to die. Your heart beats out of control; you become disorientated, dizzy, and shaky all over. After the attack, you're distraught and practically immobile. Anxiety and panic can take over your life if you let it. Once you've experienced an attack, you are never the same. You live in constant fear of having another one, which causes you to start avoiding, which in turn, starts a downhill spiral of no return.

Anxiety and panic can make you do the craziest things. Once, during a severe attack, I actually stopped a plane on the runway.

My Crazy Attack

I was on my way to Las Vegas with my mother. My mom would get a week's vacation every June and take the girls and me away. This particular summer she wanted to go to Las Vegas. My mother-in-law agreed to watch the children, and I knew my mother wanted to go, so I agreed just to make her happy.

It was my responsibility to book the trip. My mother insisted on treating us, but I knew that she really couldn't afford it, and that she had probably saved all year. It was that reason that compelled me to tell the travel agent that I wanted the cheapest deal she could find. Big mistake! Huge!

I was not fond of flying, and felt anxious weeks before the trip. We had a chartered flight with Capitol Airlines, which has since gone out of business. Everything seemed fine until we approached the plane and my mother started to complain. Mind you, she didn't know I was suffering from panic attacks. I never told her what was going on with me. How could I? I didn't understand it myself.

Nothing makes sense with this disorder. I could go on a plane, or so I thought, but find it hard to walk down the street without feeling terrified.

"This airplane is old, it looks like it's falling apart." That was the first sentence out of my mother's mouth as we started to board. Let me remind you, NEVER say negative things to a person suffering from anxiety, it's like pouring gasoline on a burning building. We boarded the plane. The seats were tight. I prayed silently to myself, while my mother whispered tidbits of wisdom in my ear. "What kind of an airline did you book us on? The seats look worn out?" I started to sweat. I felt light headed. I prayed. "Jesus help me! Keep me calm, don't let her get to me. Give me a hand. Please!"

A heavy set gentleman sat in the seat in front of me and pushed his seat all the way back, so I could hardly move. I felt trapped, which is not a good feeling. I heard the stewardess announce "Prepare for take-off!" Then she locked the door. My mother started praying out loud. "God, get this plane off the ground." She closed her eyes and clenched the armrest. That was it, I lost it! I unbuckled my seatbelt, stood up and screamed, "Stop! I have to get off." Everyone turned around and looked at me. The stewardess tried to reason with me as I walked down the aisle towards the door. "Please Miss, control yourself. You're making the other passengers nervous." "I don't care who I'm making nervous. I have to get off!" "You can't get off now, we're about to taxi." "I don't care what you're about to do, now open that door before I make a scene!"

In an attempt to control me, the attendant threatened to keep my luggage. "You can't have your luggage if you get off now, I recommend you go back to your seat and sit down." "Keep the luggage. I don't care! Just let me off this damn plane!" "What about your mother?" I looked back at my mom who had her head down in shame. "You can keep her too! Just get me out of here!" As I approached the exit door, another attendant grabbed me by the arm. The passengers clapped and gave a sigh of relief. One passenger yelled out, "Make her sit down and shut up! She's making us late!" Everyone on the plane was mumbling and complaining. I was completely out of control by now and my adrenaline was in overdrive. I felt like I was about to have a heart attack, my heart was beating so fast. I screamed out at the top of my lungs, "Open that damn door before I kill somebody!" That did it. I was causing such a commotion that the Captain ordered me off the plane. If it were today, I would have been taken away in handcuffs and interrogated. The passengers let out a round of applause as a stewardess approached the exit door. I looked back at my mother as she gave me a look. It was a mixture of *I'm going to kill you* and *I'm so ashamed*. I gave her a look back, which read, *I don't give a damn*. I heard the engines quiet as the exit door slowly opened. My mother cried out, "Wait! I'm going with her."

You find yourself doing the craziest things during an attack. There is no reasoning, and no logic. You become a different person, almost unrecognizable. Your only thought is to escape, and God help anyone who gets in your way.

My mother looked at me with disdain as she walked towards me. "What?" I asked. "You ruined my vacation," she said. There it was. THE GUILT! I knew it! I had a sinking feeling in the pit of my stomach that I would regret this day for the rest of my life.

You are probably thinking, 'What does God have to do with all of this nonsense?' God works in mysterious ways, and I was about to find out just how mysterious.

As my mother and I disembarked, a man in a golf cart, wearing a cap with the letters TWA on it, pulled up. TWA stood for Trans-World Airlines. At the time it was one of the largest airlines in the world. He introduced himself as Jim. Jim helped my mother into the cart, and we drove off down the runway towards the terminal. He asked me to explain what had happened. I told him my tale of woe, and about the man who pushed back his seat. He listened patiently. My mother didn't look or talk to me. She simply stared straight ahead and remained stoic. When we arrived at the terminal, Jim told us to follow him. I thought we were going to jail. My mother still wouldn't look at me. The next thing I knew, he was escorting us into the VIP lounge. He told us to wait for him and said that he would be right back. My mother looked at me and said, "He must be getting the police."

The room was elegant, filled with business men in fancy suits talking on phones. A lovely young woman dressed in a maid's uniform approached us with a silver tray stacked with finger sandwiches. I looked at my mother and said: "We might as well enjoy ourselves, this could be our last meal." She giggled. "Leave it to you to get us in trouble." From that moment on, we decided to enjoy ourselves. We each took several tiny sandwiches. We were served tea in dainty cups, and water in crystal glasses. My mother was in her glory. She looked at me with a girlish grin, one I had never seen before, and said, "You did good." We both laughed. The entire situation was surreal.

I felt like everyone was watching us. We were so out of place in a room full of men. I looked like a train wreck. My clothes were wrinkled, and my hair was a mess. My mother, on the other hand, looked like she belonged. She was a classy, beautiful lady, always impeccably dressed. Her clothes weren't expensive, but she always looked high-end. I was about to shove another finger sandwich in my mouth, when Jim walked in. I figured we had overstayed our welcome, and it was time to pay the price. I stood up, ready to accept my fate, when Jim stopped me. "Where are you going?" he asked. "Aren't we going to jail?" I said. He laughed. "Whatever gave you that idea? Follow me." My mother leaned over to me and said, "I knew it was too good to be true. He's taking us to the authorities." I started shaking again.

We gave the room a quick once over, took a cookie from the young lady and followed Jim to the door. I didn't see any police waiting to greet us. I figured we'd better make a quick get away before he changed his mind. After we had thanked him for everything, I started to hail a cab. "What are you doing?" he asked. "I'm calling a taxi." Just then, a limo pulled up. Jim opened the door. My mother and I looked at each other. What a nice man, I thought. He's giving us a ride home. My mother finally spoke. "Thank you Jim, but we can't afford a limo, we'll take a taxi home." Jim pulled out two name tags. "Here, put these on." "What for?" "Don't worry. I took care of everything, now hurry up your plane is waiting." "Plane? What plane?" "Your flight to Las Vegas."

Jim ordered the driver to take us to the waiting plane and make sure we got on. My mother was beaming again. The driver escorted us to the gate. He opened the door and another gentleman drove us in a cart to the plane. It was a beautiful shiny jumbo jet. We were both in shock. No panic, no anxiety, just pure shock as we boarded. The stewardess looked at our name tags and told us to follow her. I thought I was dreaming when I heard her say "Welcome to first class." When God does things, He does them in a big way.

The trip was unbelievable. Mom and me ate, drank, giggled and laughed, the entire way. I was happy to see her having so much fun. When the pilot turned on the seat-belt sign signaling we were about to land, we looked at each other with such disappointment. We wanted to shout out "NO!"

When we arrived in Vegas, a car was waiting. I couldn't believe my eyes when I spotted our names in large bold letters on a card being held by a man in a chauffeur's uniform. My mother winked at me. "Here we go again." We had a bounce to our step as we walked towards the limo. We were like two peacocks showing off our feathers. I think my mom was a little tipsy from all the free wine she drank on the plane. We couldn't stop laughing. The driver held the door and we slid inside.

We arrived at the hotel hours before the Capitol Airline passengers. You can imagine the look of disbelief on their faces when they walked in and saw us. We just smiled and said, "Hello." The receptionist at the front desk informed us at check-in that our room wasn't ready. We had nothing to do, so we did what we do best. We got into trouble.

The hotel was shiny, glitzy, and brand new. Everything in it seemed larger than life. We stood there like Alice in Wonderland looking through the looking glass. We were mesmerized, especially when we stepped into the casino. We stared at the shiny gold slot machines that spit out money. In those days they used real coins, which made gambling more fun. The sight and sound of the bells ringing, screams of joy when people hit three cherries, dollars signs, or golden nuggets, made our mouths water. We watched as people pulled the lever and the wheel in the machine spinned around. That did it, we were off! We ran towards the first machine we could find. We were like two kids at a carnival. We kept putting money in and pulling the handle. I saw my mother rubbing the machine and talking to it. "Come on baby, you can do it. Give Momma those coins." When they finally informed us that our room was ready, we were both broke. I had to call Robert to wire us money.

I smile when I think of my mother and how much fun she had. We never did find out who Jim was. I tried. I called TWA, but to no avail. Jim had disappeared as quickly as he appeared. Those few precious days with my mom were beautiful, a true blessing. Only God can turn a panic attack into a beautiful memory.

If that strange event wasn't a miracle, I don't know what is, how else could you explain it? What are the odds of any of that happening? God uses other people to help people and answer their prayers.

Back To Reality

Panic and anxiety are serious issues, and I don't mean to make light of them. At the time of the attack, I didn't think it was so funny. Just because you suffer from anxiety, it doesn't mean you can't live a full and rewarding life. It's not easy, but you can do it.

I've traveled to six out of seven continents. I've tried my hand at everything I wanted to do, and I'm still exploring. I'm a mom and a grandmother. I've been a model, an actress, a production assistance to Skitch Henderson, and Johnny Carson's right-hand man. I'm a writer, a director, and the producer of five plays so far, two of which are musicals—all while dealing with anxiety, a learning disability, and raising two small children.

I started two successful businesses. A floral design business, and an interior design business. I even won several design awards.

I say all this not to brag, but to encourage you. If I can give you any words of advice, it would be: DO IT AFRAID! If you wait until you feel great, or smart, or perfect, to do something, YOU NEVER WILL. Just do it! Life is too short for regrets and excuses.

Here's the funny and miraculous part of my story. It's a JOKE! I'm a JOKE! I never had any of the necessary skills to do any of the things I attempted. I just did them.

Looking back, I realize it was precisely because of those anxiety attacks that I was able to follow my dreams. They forced me to think outside the box. I used whatever talent and imagination God gave me to conjure up a way to make a living. Fortunately, it always focused around something I loved to do. If I tried something and it didn't work, I tried something else.

Never let anxiety or panic rule you. Learn to use the disorder to your advantage. If you know how to bang a nail, fix things. If you know how to cook, start classes from your home. Take Paula Dean, for example: she grew an entire empire because of her agoraphobia.

※　※　※

I'm a writer who can't spell. A designer who can't draw or do fractions. I was a short plum model, and an actress who couldn't read well. A JOKE!

My mission in telling you this, is to give you hope, and most of all faith. Faith in knowing that no matter how bad it gets, or how dismal it looks, God has a plan for your life and it's a GREAT ONE.

I could never have accomplished anything if it wasn't for my faith. Mind you, it's not a perfect faith. I have doubted, cried out, disbelieved and been so far down I couldn't see a way up. I've been homeless, abandoned, and a single mom. I've been judged and even lost friends and family because of my erratic behavior.

Living with anxiety and panic is no fun. People don't get it. They can't understand why you make plans, then cancel at the last minute. Panic hits without warning. How do you explain to someone that you can't leave the house? Panic can be ruthless. It destroys relationships. Yet, I wouldn't change one minute of my life if given the choice. It's because of the disorder that I depended on God so much. I hope I have encouraged you to do the same.

When I needed a job during my decorating years, I would cry out, "Lord, I need money. I need you to send me a client." I swear on my children that the words weren't even out of my mouth and the phone rang. I had a booming design business for twenty-two years, and I never placed an ad or advertised. I simply asked and received.

Being a Mom

My greatest gift, of which I take no credit, are my children and grandchildren. Being a mother isn't easy. Being a grandmother is the best.

God knows I made mistakes as a mother. What did I know? What does anyone know? We try. We learn. We fail. We try again. Somehow, it all turns out right. I'm proud of my two daughters, not for what they have accomplished, but for who they have become, good and caring people.

It wasn't easy raising two children during those panic attacks. Trying to hide the way I was feeling was a task in itself. It was hard on the girls too, I'm sure. You just do the best you can. There is nothing else you can do.

Being a mom is the hardest job in the world, especially today when the world is a little off-kilter. Stop trying to get it right, as you never will. Just love your kids with all your heart. Give them encouragement and praise. Give them self-esteem. Then pray, pray, pray.

Teach them about a Higher power. Let them know they have a loving Father they can turn to in times of trouble. You will not always be around. Children need to know there is more to life than making money. Teach them to give. To love. To make a difference.

Grandchildren is when the fun begins. You finally get to enjoy the experience of children. There is no yelling or disciplining, only joy. Thank you God for my Lauren and Ryan. I gush with pride when I think of them. Give them lots of love. In the end, that's all that really matters.

****** Food For Thought ******

Believe! You are what you believe. So, believe you are special, created in the image of Almighty God. Believe you can do anything and you will. Use your imagination. Dream. Explore. Seek adventure. Take risks. Never settle. The world is made up of dreamers. Be one!

What God Says About Fear

Psalm 34:4
"I sought the LORD, and he heard me, and delivered me from all my fears."

8

Which Came First?

JENNIFER WAS ONLY three when I found out I had cancer. Which came first, cancer or the panic?

I know now, that the anxiety I was dealing with wasn't due to stress. It was my body trying to tell me something.

I sensed that something wasn't right, but I was convinced by doctor after doctor that it was all in my head. It became apparent that they were wrong when I lost feeling in my left leg. This time I went to one of the most prominent neurologists in New York. After examining me, he found I had lost reflexes in both my knees and ankles. He immediately put me in the hospital for tests.

I felt like I had been sent to Frankenstein's horror chamber. They put me through such horrible tests. For three exhausting days I went through sheer torture. I had spinal taps, EEG's and blood sucked out of my arm every few hours. I had things stuck in my head, needles jabbed in my back, and every few hours a group of doctors came around to poke me.

Unfortunately, back then, they didn't have the equipment we have today. No MRI or CAT scans. After extensive testing, the findings all came back negative. They convinced me once again that I was crazy, even though the reflexes never came back and I still couldn't walk. I was given Valium and sent home with a clean bill of health.

The Valium helped me through the bad attacks, but something else was going on. I could feel it. Something was seriously wrong with me, and it wasn't my nerves. It was almost impossible for me to make it through the day. My sweet little Suzanne helped by taking care of Jennifer while I tried to rest. I was taking three 5 mg. of Valium a day. I barely had enough strength to make dinner. By the time Robert got home, I was ready to collapse. I didn't want to scare my girls or Robert, so when I felt a breakdown coming on, I hid in the bedroom and cried. If my kids popped their little heads in, I would shout at them to go and play with Daddy. I didn't want them to see me crying.

It was my friend Dottie who told me to check with my gynecologist. I told her I had been there six months prior. She insisted I go anyway, so I did. My friend came to the rescue once more.

When I received the call I was stunned. It caught me off-guard when the doctor told me I had stage 2 cervical cancer. Thoughts rushed through my head. I prayed. "Dear Lord help me. I can't leave my babies. You can't allow this to happen to me." The doctors wanted to perform a hysterectomy, but that little voice inside me screamed, "No!"

In spite of everyone's objections, I went for a second opinion. My cousin Natalie told me about a Doctor Calame who had cured a young girl of ovarian cancer. I made the first appointment I could get. He said straight out that I had a 50/50 chance of recovery. He told me he would do everything in his power to save me. He explained that surgery was not an option. He recommended radiation and cobalt treatments. I took his advice and prayed it was the right choice.

❅ ❅ ❅

The treatments were antiquated compared to today's standards. I had to have a full month of radiation, then two, three-day sessions of cobalt treatments in the hospital. During those treatments, I was in isolation. I had tubes coming out of every part of my body. The nurses would come in covered from head to toe in protective gear. The treatments were hard. No one was allowed to visit me, but Robert came anyway. He would stick his face against the twelve-inch glass panel on the hospital door and mouth words to me as I lay there, incapacitated. I prayed and demanded God to heal me. I kept focusing on my children. I would fall asleep holding pictures of Jennifer and Suzanne in my hand.

Eight weeks after my last treatment, it was time to find out the results. The night before my visit to the doctor, I prayed the rosary. I told myself everything would be okay, but inside I was frightened. My father was always my good luck charm, so it was imperative that I take him with me. Unfortunately, he was more nervous than me. My entire family gathered at my house and waited with bated breath for our return.

I sat quietly staring into space as Doctor Calame opened the door. I noticed he had my chart in his hand. I felt my heart pounding. He looked me straight in the eye and said, "I think we got it." I cried. It was the first time since the diagnosis that I had allowed myself to break down in front of anyone. My tears flowed like a river. I jumped for joy, and hugged and kissed Doctor Calame and my Dad. We gave praise and thanks to God, as Doctor Calame explained that I had to follow up every six months for five years, which meant I wasn't out of the woods yet. But for now, I was elated. We couldn't wait to get home and tell the rest of the family the good news.

Months passed, and I was back to my old self again. I was given a second chance and enjoying every minute of it. I felt strong, healthy, energetic and invincible. And then in a flash...

...it all came back with a vengeance.

The dizziness, the light-headedness, the shaking and the debilitating headaches were back. Only this time, they were intensified. My symptoms were so bad that it was almost impossible for me to function. I ran to see Doctor Calame, fearing for my life. He told me that I was going through early menopause and there was nothing he could do about it. They didn't have bio-identical hormones back then, I just had to deal with it. I prayed and taught myself Baby Steps.

Baby Step 1

<u>One Day at a Time:</u> Don't try and conquer the world. Learn to overcome one day at a time. When I felt sick, which was most of the time, I prayed. "God, please get me through this day." And He did.

Losing hormones at such a young age is a challenge. The body is trying constantly to correct a problem it can't fix. It's your job to convince yourself with positive self-talk and action that you're okay, healthy, and in control. It's easier said than done. Thank God for Valium. It saved my life. Drugs are not the answer, but if it wasn't for the Valium I would have stayed in bed all day.

Mind you, I still had the responsibilities of running a home and taking care of two small children, while keeping my husband happy. Robert had no idea what I was going through and I didn't want to burden him, a monumental task when you feel like you're going to collapse. I just took one step at a time and concentrated on the task at hand.

Baby Step 2

<u>Be Kind To Yourself:</u> Start by doing what you can do, when and how you can do it. I started with trying to leave the house. It sounds crazy, but when you feel like you can't stand up and your head is pounding, it's easier to stay put. I taught myself what today is called Cognitive Therapy, which is repeating the same task over and over until you feel at ease.

My family had no idea about the devastating side effects I was going through. I put on makeup and fixed my hair, and acted like I was fine. On the outside, I looked good, but inside I was a mess. My only concern was to keep things running smoothly. I established a daily routine and made sure we ate healthy meals full of veggies, fruit and lean protein. I avoided caffeine, chocolate, and sweets of any kind. I prayed through out the day. When I felt disheartened or down, I would remind myself that I was not alone and that a Higher Power was watching over my family and me.

Baby Step 3

<u>Keep Moving Forward</u>: It was hard for me to walk without feeling that sick, light-headed sensation, but I knew, if I held onto my children, I would be alright. My little girls saved my life. I held Jennifer in my arms, grabbed Suzanne's little hand and took a step. After mastering walking without falling (the dizziness had become a familiar friend), I decided to conquer shopping. Prior to that, I had my food delivered and bought clothes from catalogues. There was no online shopping back then, thank God, or else I would never have left the house. I was on my way to becoming agoraphobic. I couldn't allow that to happen.

We lived in Brooklyn where everything was within a ten-minute radius from my house. I wouldn't dare go near a mall as it was too big and confusing.

Instead, I chose whatever store was the closest. After I had conquered the mom and pop stores in the neighborhood, I decided it was time to try going to the mall. It was like a scene out of a horror movie. First, I would have to find a parking spot directly in front of the entrance. I had to be able to see my car, in case I needed to rest and retreat. I circled for what seemed like forever. After I finally found a space, I now had to muster up the courage to get out of the car and go inside. I took a deep breath, grabbed my girls and ventured out.

As I approached the entrance to the mall, I started to shake and feel dizzy. I felt fearful of passing out, so I took refuge in the car. At that point, I just wanted to go home. I composed myself, and tried again. It was mentally and physically exhausting.

I knew that the children didn't understand, so I made a game out of it. "See if you can guess how long it takes Mommy to run back to the car." That behavior continued until I felt in control. I accomplished that by teaching myself to stop, pray, and wait for the panic attack to pass. It always did.

Baby Step 4

<u>Build Self-Esteem</u>: Next on my agenda, was to do something that would make me feel better, and more in control. I was determined not

to let this condition rule me. I knew I had to stop thinking about what I couldn't do and start thinking about what I could. I also knew I had to make money.

Silk flowers were big at the time, so I decided to make floral arrangements. My cousin Augie drove me around to different vendors to buy flowers and the materials I needed. I had no idea what I was doing, I just started experimenting and putting arrangements together which I thought were pretty. People seemed to like my designs, so I started giving parties in my home. I invited a few friends, who brought their friends, and before I knew it, I had a floral design business. I went from giving parties to teaching classes twice a week in my house. When I felt sick I just popped a pill to stabilize myself and continued to work.

Baby Step 5

<u>Step Out Of Your Comfort Zone:</u> I knew I had to expand the radius I felt safe in. I prayed for an answer. That answer came in the form of an announcement during Sunday Mass. The priest asked for volunteers to teach Confraternity of Christian Doctrine (CCD). The classes were held once a week for public school children. I jumped at the chance.

Can you imagine me, a high school drop out with a learning disability and an anxiety problem, teaching? Suddenly my mother's words filled my thoughts. "You can do anything you want if you put your mind to it."

I reminded myself of the promise I made to God and to Saint Jude if I was healed from cancer. I promised I would do something to give back. In essence it's Jesus who heals, but it was Saint Jude who interceded on my behalf. CCD was my way of paying it forward.

As my body started to get used to not having hormones, and the Valium kicked in, I began to feel better. The CCD classes were a great help in my recovery. I loved teaching and working with children. They were so eager to learn and a joy to be around. They made me forget about my problems and focus on them.

Volunteering is one of the greatest gifts you can give yourself. I taught classes for ten years and loved every minute of it. My family also donated to Saint Jude's Children's Hospital. I owed Saint Jude big time. It wasn't the last time he came to my rescue...

※　※　※

... many years later I received a call. Saint Jude was summoned once more. My father was dying. I had lost my mother nine months earlier, and I was beside myself. My dad at the time was living with his sister in Florida. He was due to come up for a visit when he was diagnosed with pneumonia. The doctors informed my aunt that they would have to remove the fluid around his lungs. They told her it was a simple procedure. The next thing I knew, my aunt was on the phone telling me to get to Florida fast, as he was dying. During the surgery, something went wrong and the doctor removed one of his lungs. I called my brother and he was on the next plane to Florida. He found my father on life support. They explained to Michael that something had happened during surgery and if they didn't remove his lung he would have bled to death. It made no sense. My father had never had any trace of cancer. His lungs were healthy. They simply screwed up. They told us it was only a matter of time before he passed. My father was 78 at the time.

I was frantic. I couldn't lose my father, so I did what I do best, I prayed to God and Saint Jude. I'm not a believer in long-winded prayers, but this time I had to pull out all the stops. I made a novena: a special prayer for intercession, which is said for nine consecutive days. I swear to you on all that is holy, that on the ninth day of the novena, my father who was given up for dead, woke up and was taken off life support.

When my brother called to tell me the good news, I ran to church. I got down on my knees and thanked God and Saint Jude.

Most people relate to a Higher Power, but never acknowledge, or relate, to the saints. Why go to a saint when you can go straight to the Boss? God in His wisdom, gave us the saints as an example of what we can aspire to be. They were human just like us, suffered just like us, and sinned just like us. They didn't wake up one morning and say to themselves, "What a beautiful day, I think I'll become a saint." In fact, Saint Paul is one of our greatest saints. He is responsible for writing a large portion of the New Testament, yet, before his conversion, he persecuted Christians.

Saint Jude's Children Hospital

In the spring of 1940, Danny Thomas (who started Saint Jude's Hospital) first heard of Saint Jude from a stagehand. The man told Thomas that his wife had made a miraculous recovery from cancer after praying to the saint.

At the time Thomas was struggling to make a go of it in show business. He did some radio and nightclub work but nothing significant. When his wife Rose Marie gave birth to their third child, Thomas knew he needed to make more money. Out of desperation, he prayed to Saint Jude. He prayed for success in his profession. He promised if Saint Jude answered his prayer, he would do something special to help children.

Danny Thomas went on to become one of the most beloved and successful entertainers in show business. Thomas kept his word to his beloved saint and started The Saint Jude's Children Hospital in Memphis Tennessee. The rest is history.

Baby Step 6

<u>Challenge Yourself:</u> I was ready to move from floral design into interior design. I decided to take summer classes at the Fashion Institute of Technology (FIT) in New York for rendering and drafting. That meant driving into the city. A frightening thought, since I only traveled within my safe zone. I knew it was time to challenge myself once again.

I enlisted the help of my cousin Augie. I asked him to drive me back and forth to the city until I felt comfortable enough to do it on my own. Augie understood anxiety well; he suffered from Post Traumatic Syndrome (PTS).

The first few weeks I was a nervous wreck. Just the thought of driving to the city by myself kept me awake at night. It was summer though, which made me feel better. Besides, I had my survival kit with me in case of a sudden attack. It consisted of: water, ginger-ale, aspirin, and Pepto-Bismol. It was my first line of defense. If that failed, out came the meds. I had medicine for dizziness, headaches, fainting, and panic. I also had a supply of goodies to keep my sugar level stable. I was a walking arsenal.

Anxiety and panic are so debilitating that the fear of having another attack keeps you a prisoner. I was determined to break my chains and fight back anyway I could.

When I got to FIT, the first thing I did was familiarize myself with my surroundings. I checked all the exits in case I had to get out of the building fast. When you're fighting to breathe you don't have time to ask for directions. I took the stairs instead of the elevator. I walked up four flights of steps, convincing myself that it was good exercise. By the time I got to the class, I felt mentally and physically drained. Then I had to sit there and try to comprehend what the professor was teaching. A frightening thought since I find it difficult to understand new things. I wanted to run, but instead, I put on a brave face, took a leap of faith, opened the door and sat down.

I did whatever I had to do to get the job done. In actuality, I was fighting for my sanity, refusing to let panic rule me. I was determined to live life to the fullest. I later learned that I was also dealing with epilepsy. My neurologist told me after the diagnosis that Valium was one of the older drugs used for the condition. She made me understand that my symptoms were caused by mini short-circuits in the brain. Between epilepsy and the hormones, it's no wonder I was in such a state. But at least now, it all made sense.

I worked hard to get good grades. I practiced drafting and worked on my rendering project every night after school, instead of enjoying the summer with my family.

At the end of two arduous months of hard work the results were in. The grades were posted on a board outside the classroom. I squeezed myself in between my classmates to take a peek. There, on the board for everyone to see, was my name, with a C- next to it.

I felt shame rush over me, while memories of high school flooded my thoughts. I stood there mesmerized. My professor, who happened to be passing by, noticed me standing there in a daze, and he decided to impart a word of wisdom upon me. He basically told me to find another career. I had the same thing happen to me in high school when my homeroom teacher decided to read my report card out loud to the class. I virtually failed almost every subject. I wanted to die. I was so humiliated. That's why I quit school.

My head was spinning after Professor Feldman's discouraging remarks. I started to shake. I was having a panic attack and I couldn't breathe. I ran out of the building gasping for air. Once outside, I sat on the steps and cried my eyes out.

❄ ❄ ❄

Three years later, I sat at a luncheon given by the Chamber of Commerce to receive my first "Excellence in Design Award."

Through sheer will and determination, I designed and decorated the Staaten Catering Hall on Staten Island. It was a huge project costing over six million dollars, and I had the guts to bid on it.

The one thing I took away from those classes, proved to be invaluable. I learned the right terminology, which made me look like I knew what I was talking about. I couldn't pass a test, but I had lots of creative and exciting ideas on how to make a space look beautiful.

The job consisted of designing five catering rooms: a ballroom, a bridal room, a bar/lounge, four bathrooms and a massive lobby. I was excited and scared at the same time. I couldn't draw, but I could read an Architectural drawing and was good at communicating my ideas. When I met with the architect and builder, I explained my vision. I brought samples of floors, finishes, paint, and fabrics. I made a board showing pictures of designs I love for each space. I did my homework. I made sure I looked professional and had a friendly disposition. Little did they know I was shaking inside. I prayed every night for the project to be a success. When I look back now, I realize how crazy I was to tackle such a massive project my first time out of the gate. The only experience I had before that, was decorating my house. I had one secret ingredient, the one that outshined the rest. My love and passion for design, and the belief that I could do it.

After the catering hall was a success, I was in high demand. I worked every job, big or small, with the same zest and enthusiasm. I would interview my client, examine the space, talk about the budget, then go to work. I designed a plan based around a fabric or wallcovering, something that inspired me. Once I had the presentation board ready, I showed it to the client. I never took anyone shopping. I just explained my vision, kept to their budget and got the job. I worked that way successfully for twenty-two years.

****** Food For Thought ******

Don't be discouraged by failure. It's the road-map to your future success. You don't have to be perfect to do something, just do it. Never let your negative thoughts discourage you. Keep on keeping on! Never give up! Have faith in yourself and faith in your Creator. Then take baby steps.

Never listen to anyone who tells you not to follow your dreams. Follow them anyway. Think positive. Envision them. The only failure is not trying. Listen to that still small voice (Spirit) that plants seeds of success and a dream in your heart. Go for it, knowing that God will guide and strengthen you on your journey. Remember, everything starts with an idea, a thought, or desire. Never let fear stop you or get in the way. Live with passion! Believe! Then hold on tight because you're in for the ride of your life.

Martin Luther King

If you can't fly then run.
If you can't run then walk.
If you can't walk then crawl.

People Who Failed And Never Gave Up

Abraham Lincoln
Albert Einstein
Steve Jobs
You!

Note

Make sure that if you suffer from anxiety or panic, you investigate it further. Don't just assume it's your nerves. I truly believe, based on my experience, that the body is trying to tell you something, so listen carefully to it. Don't just pop pills. Search for an answer and pray for guidance. Ask Spirit to help you find out what's wrong. He will. Listen to Him.

9

That Still Small Voice

SEPTEMBER 11, 2001, was one of the worse days in the history of America, and yet, it brought out the best in people. Why? Why would complete strangers run to help each other instead of running the other way? It didn't matter what color, race, sex, or religion you were. We were all just brother helping brother.

I believe it's because God made us, and He made us good. Our basic instinct is to do good, not evil. It doesn't mean we don't do bad things. Since the beginning of time, a battle between good and evil has raged. Have you ever felt like you are being torn apart between the two? I'm sure you have. We all have. If it weren't so, then why do we feel guilty if we hurt someone? Where did that emotion come from?

What about the still small voice that lives inside you? You know, the voice that talks to you. The voice that tells you "haven't you had enough cake?" Or "maybe you should be exercising more?" You know the voice. The one that warns you of impending danger. It alerts you to run, watch out, or go home. That voice is Spirit.

I've heard that voice many times. I know when a person I haven't seen in a while pops into my head, it's time to give them a call. I know, because Spirit keeps repeating their name.

I remember one day, my mother who lived downstairs from me, gave me her famous whistle, signaling that she was coming up for a visit. My immediate thought was, 'oh no, not now.' It was a hectic time for me. My design business was booming and I had appointments back-to-back. Then I heard Spirit infiltrate my thoughts. It said clear as day, "Spend time with your mother. You're not going to have her around much longer."

I knew from prior experience to listen to that voice. Every time I didn't, I had regretted it. I decided to take my mother with me that hectic afternoon. It turned out to be a very special day. And one that I will never forget. My mom was suffering from colon cancer. I didn't realize then how bad she was. I took her for ice cream, her favorite treat, and one of the few things she could tolerate. I ran into each appointment while she waited in the car. She was happy to hang with me, and I was glad to be with her. We talked and laughed. Two weeks later, she was gone. I never saw it coming. If I didn't listen to Spirit's warning, I would have missed out on a beautiful memory.

The same thing happened with my father. He was visiting my brother at the time of this occurrence. God's grace allowed us to have him with us for another year after his lung debacle. I used to call my dad at 5 p.m. on the dot every night. We had a set time because he went to bed at 7 p.m. One night, I was running late with clients and didn't arrive home until 8 p.m. I was exhausted. Suddenly, I remembered I had to call my father. I picked up the phone to call when Robert said, "It's late. Call him tomorrow or you'll wake him up." I put the phone down. Then I heard Spirit in a resounding voice say "Call him." At 9:45 p.m. I finally gave in. I thought I'd just leave a message. I was surprised when my father answered the phone and said he was waiting for my call. We talked for a while. Then he said, "I love you baby." I told him, "I love you too dad." Those were the last words we said to each other. At 4:50 a.m. I got the call from my brother that God had taken him home.

Spirit is God within us. He is distinguishable from all the other chatter we have floating around in our head. His voice is constantly filling us with good, positive, comforting, inspiring, and loving thoughts. He is never negative, demanding or condemning. He helps us and sometimes warns us.

Did you know that our brain produces as many as 50,000 thoughts per day? That's according to the National Science Foundation. A huge 95 percent of these thoughts are repetitive. They reflect our mindset. If you have a negative mindset that is always telling you that you can't, then you can't. In short, if you hold on to limiting beliefs, and negative thoughts, it is most likely that you will accept limited results in your life. That is why it is imperative to think constructive, positive thoughts and discard the negative ones. Think winning thoughts and you will have a positive, productive life.

Spirit has been my guidance system for as long as I can remember. He is the reason behind every creative thought I've ever had. Believe me, out of the 50,000 thoughts I think each day, my self-talk is 75 percent negative. I have to work hard at lifting myself up, and I fight constantly to put positive thoughts in my head. It's not easy, but with practice, you can do it.

Start with exercising daily gratitude. List everything you are grateful for. Do it for thirty days, and it will become ingrained in your subconscious. (I'll explain how in Part II.)

❋　❋　❋

Once, I kept hearing "get out of the market." I remember it clearly. It was Spirit. The feeling was so intense that it woke me up in the middle of the night. I know nothing about stocks and the market, that's why Robert and I hired an investment company. I convinced my husband that something was up and we had to move our money fast. He was reluctant at first, but after much deliberation, he contacted our money manager. The next obstacle was getting our manager to agree with our decision. He vehemently objected to us pulling everything out of the market and going into certificates of deposits, even though they were paying good interest rates at the time. We insisted. It was July, 2008, when this happened—two months later the market crashed. Divine intervention. Spirit knew we needed the money to activate God's plan. That's why He protected us from losing any of our holdings.

※　※　※

I've been blessed to say goodbye to many of my loved ones because of Spirit. My cousin Carol who I adored, my mother and father, Augie my beloved cousin, and my precious friend Dottie.

Dottie and I lived far from each other, but we were always in tune. We usually talked twice a week since her diagnosis of lung cancer. I never bothered her on chemo days, yet this one particular night, Spirit told me to call her.

I knew something was terribly wrong when she answered the phone. Her voice seemed weak. She was ready to check out, I could tell. My friend had a way of making everyone laugh no matter how dire the situation. She brought fun, laughter, and light into the world. This night was different. I was alarmed at her reluctance to speak to me. To tell me what was going on. I kept insisting until she finally broke down and said she was in the ER.

I wanted to get to her, but she stopped me. Her concern was for me as she lay there dying. She told me how much she loved my family and me. I told her the same and begged her to hang on. Selfishly, I didn't want to lose her. She asked me to tell Pat, our dear friend, that she loved her and to say goodbye. When I hung up, I immediately called Pat. She was blessed to catch her in time. I was on my way to the hospital when I received the call.

My story isn't a story about loss, it's a story about life and miracles. It's about the blessings that are open to everyone. It's about love and Spirit.

I'm not anyone special or necessarily intuitive. I'm just open. Be open too! I don't want you to miss the opportunities that Spirit presents every day. Allow yourself time to shut down, slow down, be still. He is there. Waiting. It's not always big things that Spirit tells you. Most of the time it's little things, like 'don't park there you'll get a ticket, stop texting while you drive, or, he's not the one for you.' Spirit guides us in many ways. Sometimes it's a feeling. A knowing.

I had just finished a huge design project. I was in charge of designing two 10-story apartment buildings called The Fountains. The Fountains were luxury apartment buildings with a view of the golf course and Clove Lake Park on Staten Island. The project took almost two years to complete. As I walked to my car, I suddenly had the urge to look back at the completed buildings. As I stood there staring, I had this overwhelming feeling that it was time to move on.

That day, I walked away from a design business I loved, which generated a significant income, and never looked back. God had something bigger in mind for me. I had no idea what, but I knew I was about to find out.

****** Food For Thought *******

Follow your heart. If Spirit demands attention, give it to Him. Meditate. Ask for guidance and wisdom, then receive it. Keep asking for what you want until you get it. You will. Dream big dreams! Learn to trust.

When your heart leaps for joy while doing something you love, it's a sign that you're on the right path. When you feel the sudden urge to connect with someone—do it. Know that it's Spirit talking to you. Never take anything for granted, let Spirit guide your path. If you do, you will discover happiness, joy, and fulfillment. Go for it!

10

Michael's Miracle

ANSWERED PRAYERS COME in all shapes and sizes. They show up when you least expect them, and not always in the way you expected.

Michael was gay. He never came out and said it, we just knew. We loved him unconditionally and felt sad that he didn't confide in us. Maybe it was because of the crazy way we grew up, or the fact that he was a Green Beret. I'm not sure. I only know it was hard on him. We grew up in a time when being gay was frowned upon. I worried about my brother. We would hang out and have long talks whenever he was around. I know he struggled with his sexuality and felt isolated. It broke my heart. I tried to convince him to have faith and to turn to God whenever he felt like that. Michael rejected the idea. I know he loved and believed in God, but he felt like an outsider. I wanted my brother to know the God I knew and depended on so much. A Father who loves us unconditionally. I told him that Jesus died for all of us, not only for some of us. He just shook his head. I prayed.

Months later, I was at my friend Pat's house in Florida. I was asleep when something startled me. I sat up in bed and looked around. I noticed the clock on the night stand was showing 5:15 in the morning. I flopped back in bed and pulled the covers over my head. I tossed and turned until finally, I got up and started to get dressed. I went into the kitchen and made myself oatmeal. As soon as the spoon touched my tongue, I thought to myself, 'where am I going at this hour in the morning?' I started to go back to bed when I felt the sudden urge to go to Mass. I couldn't figure out why, I just knew I had to go...

❀ ❀ ❀

...then a strange thing happened, I found myself waking up every day for two weeks, at exactly 5:15. No matter how hard I tried, I couldn't break the routine. My friend thought there was something wrong with me. One morning she caught me as I was about to sneak out the door. "Where do you go every morning," she asked. "I go to Mass. I have no idea why. I just go." She shook her head, and went back to bed.

One day, during Mass, I heard this song; it was so incredibly beautiful and touching that it gave me goose bumps. I knew instinctively, for whatever reason, that song had something to do with my brother, and me going to church. I searched the hymn book for its name but couldn't find it. After the ceremony, I approached the music director to inquire about the song. We chatted for a while. He told me it was the first time he had played the song at Mass. He said it made him think of his brother. At that moment, I knew Spirit was up to something. I couldn't figure out what, but I trusted and went with my instincts...

❀ ❀ ❀

...which led me in a round-about way to writing. *The Saga Continues...*

How I Got Into Writing

If someone told me I'd be a writer, I would have laughed. I never had any intention or desire to write, however, when God has a plan, watch out. He replaced my love for design with a passion for writing. It happened the day I looked back at the two apartment buildings I had just completed and knew, it was time to move on.

God's plan for my life didn't just happen, it came in cycles. He guided me step by step towards His ultimate goal. A goal I would never have set for myself.

For a while, I was in limbo and wondered if I had made the right decision about giving up my business. Whenever I felt like that in the past, I would volunteer for some organization. It was time to get my mind off of myself, and on to someone else. I turned to Crossroads.

Crossroads is a charitable organization that helps single mother's get back on their feet. I became very close with two of the mom's, who are now like daughters to me. I enjoyed working with the organization but something was still missing, I could sense it.

I needed something more, something to occupy my mind while I waited for Spirit. On a whim, I decided to take a set-design class at HB studio in the city. HB is primarily a school for acting, but when I looked up its courses online, I found set-design. I thought it might be fun and decided to give it a try. When I went to register for the class, I discovered that they offered no such design class. How could that be? I was puzzled, so not to look stupid, I took an acting class instead.

To my astonishment, I enjoyed every minute of the class. I made great friends and loved doing scenes, and monologues. It was exciting to work with scene partners and then perform the scene in front of the class. I was hooked! Acting is a great comfort, as it forces you to focus on the moment.

A city I had once dreaded, now became my best friend. Suzanne was working as a buyer for one of the largest retailers in New York, and Jennifer was living her dream as an actress. Whenever our schedules permitted, we would meet for lunch. One afternoon, Jen met me after school. She was working on Rebecca Miller's new film called, *Enter Fleeing*. Jennifer said they were looking for someone to play her mother in the movie. She insisted I go for the audition. I cherished the idea of working with my daughter. I thought it would be fun, so I agreed.

Rebecca cast me in the role, and just like that, I had an agent. Larry Taube from the Gersh Agency agreed to take me on because of Rebecca's recommendation. Meanwhile, during filming, Rebecca ran off with Daniel Day-Lewis! They met during the filming of *The Crucible* and fell in love. That was the end of her movie, but the beginning of a new adventure for me.

The Gersh Agency started sending me out on calls. It was exciting and frustrating at the same time. Finally, I booked my first film called *Tavern On Jane*. I played the part of the other woman. I loved going on auditions, but hated the fact that I was always cast as the 'Mistress.'

One of the most memorable auditions was for *The Sopranos,* one of the highest-rated shows on HBO at the time. It was both exciting and scary. I had to read in front of David Chase the producer, and a room full of casting people. It was nerve-wracking to say the least. I was reading for the part of Junior Soprano's girlfriend (played by Dominic Chianese.) The dialogue was direct and sexually explicit, but I managed to pull it off. The next day, I got a call from my agent saying that casting was holding my time (which meant they wanted me for the part.) I was shocked because usually, you get several callbacks before they make the final decision. I found out a few days later that it was between myself and another actress. The part involved some nudity which was beyond my comfort zone. I prayed that the other actress would get the part, and she did.

I wanted to be more than fluff, that's when I decided to write something for myself. I started out writing a scene for me and my scene partner Marguerite. Marguerite and I were paired together our first day at HB. We began as strangers and ended up as best friends. I wrote a comedy skit about two women looking for love. We tried it out in class, and everyone seemed to enjoy it. At lunch, I told Marguerite I was going to write a sitcom for us. Unfortunately, I never got the chance. Marguerite had to leave New York because her green card had expired. Today my beautiful friend is an activist for peace and stability in Venezuela her homeland. I continued to write.

❋ ❋ ❋

I know nothing about writing having taken only one, two-hour class with Ellen Sandler of *Everybody Loves Raymond* fame. She was one of the principal writers for the show. It was an interesting class, but how much can you learn in only two hours? Fortunately, I was familiar with formatting a script from reading so many at school, and on auditions. I learned the rest from doing. When I felt inspired, I turned on the computer and started to write. I had no plan, only an idea. Once I began, I allowed the story to take me where it wanted to go. I was on my way. After my first play was completed, I formed my production company and named it Rylor Productions.

Opening Night

I was excited to see my work in action. I forgot about acting and concentrated on casting and directing. The Psychic Cafe was my first attempt at writing a play, and I was performing it in front of a live audience. I sat in the control booth with the technician, and directing the light and sound cues. I was shaking from head to toe until I heard the first chuckle. To my surprise The Psychic Cafe turned out to be a huge success. I was thrilled to know I could make people laugh. It made me feel that in some small way, I had made a contribution. Little did I know, it was all part of a Divine plan.

After Psychic Cafe's debut, I couldn't stop writing. I wrote, produced, and directed four other plays. The latest being, Love, Sex, and Menopause which recently finished a hit run. I was hooked on the laughter.

I do the strangest things, maybe it's because of the short-circuit in my brain? For instance, for my second play Surprise, I wrote the play, after it was all finished and ready to go up, I kept hearing this melody playing in my head. I couldn't get it out of my mind, so, at the last minute, I decided to turn Surprise into a musical. Who does things like that? Strange the way my mind works. I would whistle the melody to

Robert, he would strum it on his guitar, then I'd write the lyrics based on the script, and the musical was born.

During the casting for Surprise, I found Joey. Joey could act, sing and write songs. I cast him as Johnny, the lead in the play. I also made him part of the team. Together, Robert, Joey, and I wrote the score for Surprise.

The next step was the recording studio. That's how we found Carlos. Carlos is a genius at mixing sounds, plus he had a fantastic studio with all the latest equipment. It was a match made in heaven.

It was an exhilarating experience to watch the development of a simple melody turn into a song. After Carlos had finished adding the sound of strings, woodwinds, brass, and percussion to the score, the singers sounded as though they had a full-blown orchestra behind them. Amazing!

My productions all made money which went to charity and to cover expenses. My focus was never on the money. My primary concern was testing the show, getting the audience reaction, and giving my actors a chance to showcase their talent. Acting is the only profession you do for free in the hope of being discovered. I wanted to give them that chance.

I only ran a show for a few days. It was too expensive to keep it running. Who knew that's what you're supposed to do? You keep a show up long enough to get a buzz. You invite agents and managers, with the hopes of getting it picked up. I'm the only producer who pulls a hit show just as its gaining momentum. Stupid!

After Surprise opened, my neighbor Nancy offered me money. She said she had received an inheritance and wanted to invest in the play. She loved the music and couldn't stop singing the songs. She asked me how much money I needed to get it going. I like a jerk, said, "Thanks, Nan, but it would take millions."

Then Ira, a Hedge Fund manager tried to help me. He also loved the play and offered backing. A director at the Hallmark Channel became interested in the script and wanted to turn Surprise into a movie. I was back and forth to LA for months. It was overwhelming.

I had a producer, Suzanne Corso, offer me a showcase at Ars Nova for one of my plays. Ars Nova is one of the hottest clubs in Manhattan. It's where agents go to discover new talent. I turned it down. In every situation, I found some excuse to sabotage the project and myself. Why?

God sent me so many opportunities. The last offer was for my production of Love, Sex & Menopause. I never followed up. I even had a Theater company offer to put up Surprise. I refused again, and again, and again.

❈ ❈ ❈

The bottom line, I didn't feel my work was good enough, that I was good enough. I was scared of the responsibility, and for the first time in my life, I doubted.

❈ ❈ ❈

Our Father is a God of many chances. He knew I had no idea what I was doing. He also knew I didn't understand or see the vision He had in mind...

❈ ❈ ❈

...Back to my brother Michael and the song that kept haunting me.

I couldn't figure out why this song was so important. Then I heard Spirit say "turn it into a play." Not Too Far From Here is the song I heard in church that day in Florida. The song is about hurting people.

I sat down at my computer and started to write. I listened to the song as I wrote. My intention was to write about a society too busy to see the reality and suffering of others, but God had other plans. It was as though the writing took on a life of its own. Suddenly, the direction changed in midstream and turned into the adventures of three inner-city kids, one of which just happens to be gay. The story takes you on a roller coaster ride with many twists and turns until it reaches its climactic and surprising ending.

Not Too Far From Here, is quite a departure for me. It's my first attempt at writing something other than comedy. The focus of the play is love, acceptance, and survival. It's about beating the odds.

Note

Not Too Far From Here the play, and subsequent short film, is currently in production. It is dedicated to my brother Michael.

An Unexpected Turn

We never know when we wake up what the day has in store. We automatically take it for granted that everything will go as planned. Then something unexpected happens, and your to-do-list goes out the window.

Several weeks prior, I was at a production meeting when Joey received a call that his uncle was dying. As he was leaving to go to the hospital, one of the actors yelled after him to say the Divine Mercy prayer over his uncle. I have heard people saying the prayer in the chapel, but I never gave it much thought. In fact, I was annoyed at the interruption and left.

At 2:20 a.m. on April 30th, 2015, I had a life-altering experience. The day started out as usual. Only God knew what the next several hours would reveal.

It was a restless night. I couldn't sleep so I turned on the television. At the time, I had an answering machine. When a call came in, the number would flash on the TV. When I saw Michael's number appear, my heart started to pound. I knew something was wrong. I was afraid to pick up the phone. I held my breath until the phone stopped ringing. I was frightened to call back. I didn't want to hear what I already knew. My brother was in trouble. I started to pray. "Dear God, please! No! Not my brother please!"

I finally got the courage to call back. Jurgen, his partner, was hysterical. Michael was dying. An infected cat had bitten him, and the infection was running rampant. He wasn't expected to make it through the night. I immediately asked if he had called a priest. I wanted my brother to make peace with God. Jurgen told me Michael emphatically said no, and he wasn't going against his wishes. I rushed him off the phone and told him to start praying. He said there was no hope and that Michael's organs were shutting down. Jurgen is a hospice nurse, so he knew what he was talking about, "I don't care!" I yelled into the phone and hung up.

I got down on my knees. The television was still on, and I must have hit the button on the remote because suddenly the image of Divine Mercy appeared. It was 3 a.m. I prayed. I cried out to God to save him. I couldn't bear to lose my brother. I needed him. I asked the Blessed Mother to intercede for me. I begged. I was hysterical. I cried out to God. "If you are the God of Mercy, I beg You to save my brother!"

The phone was ringing again. This time I answered. It was Jurgen shouting into the phone "Whatever you're doing keep on doing it! Michael just turned the corner." I kept praying to Divine Mercy and reciting the prayer they were saying on the television.

It was 5:30 in the morning when Jurgen called back. He said that the doctors told him to go home and rest. Michael seemed to be getting better. I gave thanks and fell on the bed, exhausted. I was sobbing as I closed my eyes.

On May 1, 2015, at 3:30 p.m. my brother passed away almost thirteen hours after the doctors had given up hope.

The Miracle

The miracle is in his death. During those thirteen hours, I believe Michael encountered Jesus. I believe with all my heart that the love and mercy Michael felt during those hours wiped away his anger, and he surrendered to His Heavenly Father. When Jurgen arrived at the hospital, Michael was still alive. A priest was at his side. Michael looked at Jurgen with an accepting glance, closed his eyes and let go.

Jurgen said he had never seen anyone die the way Michael did. As a hospice nurse, he saw people die every day. Most of the time they struggled. It natural to fight for your life. Let's face it, no one wants to die. They are put on a morphine drip to help with the transition. Michael not only surrendered willingly, but he declined any drugs. He simply closed his eyes and went to sleep.

Jurgen said that he died with a smile on his face, a glow, and a look of peace. He couldn't stop talking about how his partner of 33 years looked. The next morning, just to reassure himself, he went to the hospital to say his last goodbye. He said Michael had that same glow, and look of peace.

❊ ❊ ❊

It all makes sense to me now. God had answered my prayer. I prayed that Michael would come to know God's love and he did. I realize that the play *Not Too Far From Here* was given to me as a way of communicating to others, Jesus's love and mercy for all those who feel unloved or unaccepted. Finding Divine Mercy at a meeting was not an accident. Hearing the prayer in the chapel was a gift. Going to Mass every day in Florida was not a strange occurrence. It was all part of the Divine plan. A picture of mercy and love.

After Michael's miracle, I needed to find out all I could about the story behind Divine Mercy. This is what I discovered...

Divine Mercy

The message of Divine Mercy was given to us by JESUS HIMSELF, when he appeared to a simple nun Sister Faustina (Helen Kowalska) on February 22, 1931, in her convent in Kracow, Poland. Sister Faustina documented the events in her Diary. This is a page from that Diary:

> "In the evening, when I was in my cell, I became aware of the Lord. Jesus clothed in a white garment. One hand was raised in blessing, the other was touching the garment at the breast. From the opening of the garment at the breast there came forth two large rays, one red and the other pale. In silence I gazed intently at the Lord; my soul was overwhelmed with fear, but also with great joy. After a while Jesus said to me, 'paint an image according to the pattern you see, with the inscription: Jesus, I trust in You.'"
>
> "The pale ray stands for the Water which makes souls righteous; the red ray stands for the Blood which is the life of souls.

These two rays issued forth from the depths of My most tender Mercy at that time when My agonizing Heart was opened by a lance on the Cross....Fortunate is the one who will dwell in their shelter, for the just hand of God shall not lay hold of him."

The Divine Mercy Promise

"I promise that the soul that will venerate this image will not perish. I also promise victory over its enemies already here on earth, especially at the hour of death.

I myself will defend it as My own glory. (Diary 48)

I am offering people a vessel with which they are to keep coming for graces to the fountain of Mercy.

That vessel is this image with the signature, Jesus, I trust in You."
(Diary 327)

Note

It is of particular importance to pray the Divine Mercy prayer at 3 a.m. and 3 p.m. The time of our Lord's suffering and death. It is equally important to say it for a sick and dying loved one.

Divine Mercy Prayer

Eternal Father, I offer You the Body and Blood, Soul and Divinity of Your Dearly Beloved Son, Our Lord Jesus Christ, in atonement for our sins and those of the whole world.

For the sake of His sorrowful Passion, have mercy on us and on the whole world.

I never mourned my brother. I knew he was with God, and at peace. My only regret was that I didn't listen to Spirit when he told me to call him. It was the same day of the incident. I was too tired. I figured I'd call him the next day. The next day he was gone.

A Strange Happening

Almost a year after my brother's passing, Jurgen called to tell me he saw Michael. At first, he thought it was a dream, then he realized he was having an out of body experience. He was sitting on the sofa watching television when suddenly, he was hovering above the room looking down at his body. He recalls thinking how old and worn out he looked. He was frightened at first because he found himself in a blue haze, and then he saw my brother. He wanted to go to him, but Michael held out his hand (as if to say no). Michael told Jurgen that he had to go back. He told him he would be watching over him, and that Jurgen would be with him soon. As he moved towards Michael, he found himself back on the sofa.

Jurgen later told me, that Michael looked young and healthy, and had the same glowing smile on his face.

I had a Memorial Mass for my beloved brother on September 19, 2015, his birthday. It is said, when one door closes, another one opens. That day at the Memorial, unbeknownst to me, another miracle was about to take place...

Note

Saint Pope John Paul II declared SR. MARY FAUSTINA KOWALSKA, of Divine Mercy, a Saint on Sunday, April 30, 2000, at the Vatican. He also visited her Shrine in Poland.

****** Food For Thought ******

Don't take the people in your life for granted. I lost the opportunity to say goodbye to my beloved brother because I was too tired to make a call. Don't make the same mistake.

If you think of someone, reach out to them. Remember to say "I love you." Call a parent you haven't spoken to in a while. Hug a child, a friend, your significant other. Acknowledge a homeless person with a simple hello. Stop, look, and listen, long enough to enjoy the little things in life. Give thanks to God for the day, you will never get another one like it again. Appreciate and enjoy the beauty that surrounds you. Make the world a better place with random acts of kindness. Lift someone's spirits with a compliment. Be happy!

Pray to Divine Mercy for a loved one. Believe and trust in your Heavenly Father, for He is good and gentle of heart.

11

Spontaneous Healing

The First Healing:

I HAD FALLEN badly while cleaning the floor with flip-flops on. I twisted my leg on the way down and landed hard on the kitchen tile. I got up as if nothing had happened. Days later, my left knee started to throb. I put ice on it and took pain killers. I thought it would go away on its own, but every day the pain got worse. I stopped doing my morning exercises. It was hard to walk without being in extreme pain. One morning I was at the supermarket ready to checkout my items, when the pain became so intense that I had to leave the store. It was time to see a doctor.

I went to see an orthopedic specialist referred to me by my primary doctor. The specialist examined my knee and told me I had a torn meniscus and needed surgery. I argued with him, refusing to believe I had anything more than a sprain. The results of the MRI were conclusive. It showed that my meniscus was torn.

I have trouble sleeping. Therefore, I keep the television on until I start to doze. Robert, on the other hand, is asleep the minute his head hits the pillow. This one particular night, just as I was about to close my eyes, a picture of Our Lady of Guadalupe appeared on the screen. I saw pictures of her in church before, but never knew the story behind Guadalupe. I was intently listening to her story when suddenly, the pain in my knee jolted me back to reality. I'm not a patient person and have no time for nonsense like a screwed-up knee. I had work to do, important work assigned to me by God, and it was imperative that I get started. I saw the opportunity and took advantage of it. I looked straight at Our Lady of Guadalupe's picture on the television screen and said, "If you want me to do the job, I need my legs!"

My healing was SPONTANEOUS. The excruciating pain in my left knee was gone. I touched my knee, it felt warm. I could feel the heat radiating from it. I got up and walked around, then got down on my knees (something I couldn't do before the healing) and gave thanks to God and Our Lady for healing me.

I relate this strange and magical occurrence back to the simple request I made one day at the chapel. It wasn't actually a request, it was more a question. And I knew beyond a shadow of a doubt that my healing had something to do with it. I promised to do something special for Our Lady. I knew what that was, and so did she.

I find it impossible to go any further without telling you the story behind Our Lady of Guadalupe.

The Story

On December 9th, the feast of the Immaculate Conception, Our Lady of Guadalupe appeared to Juan Diego, a poor Indian man. She appeared as a young woman surrounded by light on Tepeyac, a hill, northwest of Mexico City. The beautiful Lady identified Herself as The Mother of God.

Words From Our Lady Spoken to Juan Diego

"Know, that I am the perfect and ever Virgin Holy Mary, Mother of the God of truth through Whom everything lives. I want very much to have a little house built here for me, in which I will show Him, I will exalt Him and make Him manifest. I will give Him to the people in all my personal love, in my compassion, in my help, in my protection: because I am truly your merciful Mother, yours and all the people who live united in this land and of all the other people of different ancestries. My lovers, who love me, those who seek me, those who trust in me. Here I will hear their weeping, their complaints and heal all their sorrows, hardships and sufferings." You must go to the residence of the Bishop of Mexico and tell him that I sent you here to show him how strongly I wish him to build me a temple here on the plain; you will report to him exactly all you have seen, admired and what you have heard."

"Do not let your countenance, your heart be disturbed. Am I not here, I, who am your Mother? Are you not under my shadow and protection? Am I not the source of your joy? Are you not in the hollow of my mantle, in the crossing of my arms? Do you need anything more?"

Juan Diego immediately told the Bishop what the Lady had said to him. The perplexed bishop said he would need a sign from Heaven to comply. On Juan's next visit with the Lady, she told him to gather some flowers, which he would find at the top of the hill. Upon arriving there, he discovered by the side of an enormous rock the most beautiful gathering of white roses he had ever seen. She told him to carry the flowers in his tilma (a rough cactus fiber outer garment) to the Bishop. She strictly ordered him not to show the contents of the tilma to anyone on the way. Once there, he began to tell his story to the Bishop. He unfolded his tilma. As the Bishop, and some notable guests who happened to be present, saw what had been hidden in the tilma, they immediately fell on their knees. The flowers covered by the tilma, changed into the image of Our Lady.

The Cathedral in honor of Our Lady was built at the exact place where Diego's tilma and the Image was first seen.

The Miracle of The Image The Fabric

NASA scientists cannot explain how the image was imprinted on the tilma. There are no brush strokes or sketch marks on it. The colors actually float above the surface of the tilma at a distance of 3/10th of a millimeter (1/100th of an inch), without touching it.

In 1936, biochemist Richard Kuhn, a Nobel Prize winner in chemistry, analyzed a sample of the fabric and ascertained that the pigments used were from no known source; whether natural, animal, mineral, or vegetable.

On May 7, 1979, Americans Dr. Philip Callahan, a biophysicist and Jody B. Smith, a professor at the College Pensacola, who are both specializing in painting and members of NASA, photographed the image under infrared light and scanned it at very high resolutions. After filtering and processing the digitized images they discovered that portions of the face, hands, robe, and mantle had been painted in one step, with no sketches, or corrections, and no visible brush strokes or protective varnish.

The image still retains its original colors, despite being unprotected by any covering during the first 100 years of exposure.

Carlos Fernandez del Castillo, a gynecologist, examined the image and has determined that the gynecological measurements of Our Lady's physical dimensions indicated a woman who is pregnant. There was a black band at the waist, a sign that she is pregnant. He heard rhythmic repeating heartbeats at 115 beats per minute, the same as that of a baby.

December 22, 1981

Astronomical studies analyzed the stellar arrangement that appears in the Mantle of Our Lady. They surprisingly discovered that the stars stunningly and accurately map out the various constellations of the Mexican sky.

Even more remarkable is the "star map" on the mantle is in the reverse, providing a view of the constellations from beyond them, as would be seen looking through them towards the Earth.

Miracle Of Our Lady's Eyes

Digital enlargements of the image were made. It was discovered that the reflection in Her eyes was of the Bishop looking in astonishment. It could clearly be seen in Her pupil (only about 1/3rd inch in size), not only the minuscule human image of a bearded man, clearly identifiable in the eyes, that no artist could have painted, but all the optical imaging qualities of a normal human eye, such as light reflection, image positioning, and distortion on the cornea which are impossible to obtain on a flat surface. When the eye of Our Lady is exposed to light, the retina contracts, and when the light is withdrawn, it returns to a dilated state, the same as happens with a living eye. Our Lady's eyes have been ophthalmologically determined to be alive on the tilma!

All who have scientifically examined the image of Our Lady over the centuries confess that its properties are absolutely unique and so inexplicable in human terms that the image can only be supernatural.

※　※　※

Second Healing / two years later:

I was scheduled to film on Friday. Two days before the shoot, Robert was carrying me into the doctor's office. The pain was shooting up my leg, and my right foot was twice its usual size. I had picked up an infection at the nail salon during a pedicure. My foot was so swollen that I couldn't put pressure on it, much less walk. The doctor took one look at my foot and told me if the red mark moved up my leg to get to the emergency room immediately. He gave me antibiotics and told me to call him the next morning.

That evening, I had a fever of 102 and the pain was so intense that I screamed as Robert helped me into bed. Even the soft cotton sheet hurt as it brushed up against my swollen foot. Robert wanted to take me to the ER as instructed. I convinced him to give it another day. He put a cold cloth on my head and ran to pick up my medicine.

E channel was interested in doing a reality show around Jennifer and her bakery. Jennifer had fulfilled her first dream of becoming an actress. Her second dream was to open a gluten-free bakery after she discovered she had celiac disease. She was determined to help people, especially children. She wanted people to be able to have great desserts without the fear of getting sick. When E channel approached her to do a show about her bakery, she jumped at the chance. I had a small part in the show. I was already in several scenes and was scheduled to shoot another one on Friday.

I was frantic. There was no way I could work in this condition. When Robert left to pick up my medicine, I called the producer to explain the situation. The producer convinced me that the scene would be quick. It was the interview segment of the show and I would be sitting down. She also said she would send a car to pick me up. I couldn't let my daughter down, so I agreed.

I had to do something to try and reduce the swelling in my foot, so I decided to soak it in Epsom Salt. The only problem was, I had to get out of bed and into the bathroom to do it. I slowly and painfully maneuvered myself to the edge of the bed. As I placed my swollen foot on the floor, I screamed. The pain was excruciating. I felt like my body was on fire. I was angry and hollered out to God, "I need Your help! I need You to heal my foot! Jesus, help me please!" And just like that I was healed, again.

This healing confirmed my original suspicion, that it had something to do with the chapel. It had to be. How else could it be explained?

Whenever you are trying to bring light into the world, darkness will always try and stop you. And I was on a mission to bring in the light.

❊ ❊ ❊

When Robert arrived home with the medicine, I was standing at the kitchen counter shoving food into my mouth. "What are you doing out of bed?" He asked. "I thought you couldn't move." I told him I was fine, and that God had healed me. He looked at me like I had three heads. Then Robert leaned over and touched my forehead. I guess he figured I was delirious from the fever and hallucinating. "You're cool." I proceeded to reassure him by showing off my foot. "What happened to the swelling?" He watched me as I pranced around the kitchen, "I don't believe it. What the heck did you do to your foot?" I repeated, "I asked God to heal me, and He did." Robert sat down at the kitchen table with a puzzled look on his face, and who could blame him? He handed me the prescription bottle of pills and said, "I guess you won't be needing these anymore?"

When Jennifer heard from the producer that I had a problem with my foot, she immediately called. I reassured her that I was fine. She was concerned I might have blood poisoning and not know it. She didn't buy the healing story. She insisted I have my blood checked. She had her doctor arrange an immediate blood test. I went to the lab just to humor her. Everything was fine.

I didn't think my healings were strange. God heals His children in miraculous ways everyday. He knew I had a job to do for Him, and I needed His help to do it. It's that simple.

Hebrews 11:1
Faith is the assurance of things hoped for, the conviction of things not seen.

****** Food For Thought *******

The Blessed Mother known to some as Mary, or the Virgin Mary, is the Mother of God. She is only apparent in the Bible during Jesus's birth, death, and at the wedding of Cana, where Jesus performed His first miracle, turning water into wine at her request.

It would take several volumes for me to explain the power of the Blessed Mother. She is one of the greatest gifts from God to us. We are so lucky to have a loving Mother to watch over and protect us. To be there for us when we call.

She has visited us here on Earth many times. She comes to help, warn, inform, but most of all, to show her love, and bring us closer to her Son Jesus Christ.

Our Lady of Guadalupe is only one appearance. There have been numerous apparitions of Our Lady in almost every part of the world.

The church has officially confirmed the apparitions of Our Lady of Guadalupe, Saint-Étienne-le-Laus, Paris (Rue du Bac, Miraculous Medal), La Salette, Lourdes, Fátima, Portugal, Pontmain, Beauraing and Banneux, and Belgium.

Learn about the miracle of the children at Garabandal, and the miracle of Madjugorje, a little town in the region of Bosnia. They will excite your heart, and give you courage and hope.

*Please note: The apparitions of Garabandal and Madjugorje are currently under investigation by the Church. It has officiated the normal procedures prior to declaring the apparitions miraculous.

Prayers to The Blessed Mother

The Memorare

Hail, holy Queen, Mother of Mercy, Our life, our sweetness and our hope. To thee do we cry, poor banished children of Eve. To thee do we send up our sighs, Mourning and weeping in this valley of tears. Turn then, most gracious Advocate, thine eyes of mercy toward us, And after this our exile, show unto us the blessed fruit of thy womb, Jesus. O clement, O loving, O sweet Virgin Mary! Pray for us. O Holy Mother of God. That we may be made worthy of the promises of Christ.

The Hail Mary

Hail Mary, full of grace, the Lord is with thee; blessed are thou among women, and blessed is the fruit of thy womb, Jesus. Holy Mary, Mother of God, pray for us sinners, now and at the hour of our death. Amen.

I cried out to our Mother and she heard me. That's what mothers do. I promise, she will do the same for you!

Leap of Faith

Investigate the apparitions of the Blessed Mother that I mentioned, if for nothing else other than curiosity. I promise, you will not be disappointed.

12

The Question that Changed My Life

Summer and all is well...

WALKING ON THE beach as the sun kissed my face and the warm breeze blew gently through my hair, I thanked God for being alive. I loved jumping out of bed at the crack of dawn to get my morning exercise. It's a wondrous time of day when everything is quiet and peaceful, and the only audible sound is the movement of the waves crashing against the shore. I needed to exercise. I was bored, restless...

❀ ❀ ❀

...and had a nagging feeling that Spirit was up to something.

Suzanne was married and busy raising Lauren and Ryan. Robert was working, and Jennifer was in California making movies. I was writing and producing plays, but something was coming, I could tell.

When my friend Grace asked me to go to Paris with her, I jumped at the chance. Even though I had been to the "City of Lights" many times before, I was excited to introduce it to my friend. Besides, I needed the distraction. I was planning on leaving in a few weeks when my plans were suddenly interrupted.

It was Pat that first introduced me to the chapel—the chapel that changed my life. It is tucked away in a cozy corner on the lush, green, grounds, of the property of The Saint Paul Society. The long winding road leading up to the chapel is enchanting. It is bordered on both sides by gigantic trees whose willowy branches fold gently together forming a beautiful A-line covering. During the day when rays of sun pierce through the thick leafy covering, it feels almost magical.

As you continue along the road, you can see the lovely little white chapel in the distance. In front of it is a statue of the Blessed Mother surrounded by roses. You get the feeling as you approach the chapel that you are about to experience something extraordinary.

The focal point of the chapel is Jesus, present in the Holy Eucharist and displayed in a special holder called a monstrance.

I have come to love and depend on this little chapel. People come here to pray and worship continually throughout the day and night. Sometimes in the middle of the night when I couldn't sleep, I would go there and sit. Many miracles have come out of this chapel, one of which was about to be mine.

※　※　※

I was getting ready for Paris. We were scheduled to leave in a few days. I usually go to the chapel and say a prayer before I travel, but I was too busy racing around with last minute details. The next day, I decided to stop by on my way to the bank. It was about 4 p.m. when I finally got there. The chapel was calming. I started to pray my usual list of requests when I stopped, a feeling of sadness had come over me. I realized that all I did was ask and take. I was before the King of the Universe, and all I could think about was me.

I began to meditate on all the blessings I had received over the years. I asked myself, 'what have I given to Him?' Would I, at the end of my life come to my Saviour empty-handed? I looked at the cross and said, "What can I give to You?" I prayed not to leave this world without making a difference. I wanted my life to count for something other than me. I prayed for a safe trip, made the sign of the cross and left. When I arrived home Robert greeted me with the bad news.

The week before I was to leave, I had gone to my gynecologist for my annual checkup. She had left a message with Robert for me to call. It was not good news. My pap test had come back suspicious and my doctor wanted me to have a biopsy immediately. I told her I'd take care of it when I returned home from France. She insisted the findings were not good and it was imperative I see my oncologist right away. With regret, I canceled my trip.

The next few weeks were frightening to say the least. I needed all my strength just to keep going. Finally a break-through. The oncologist told me he didn't think the cancer had returned. He felt it was the effects of the radiation that was causing me to get a positive pap test. He gave me hormone cream and told me to see him in a month. I was relieved and scared at the same time. If this medicine didn't work, I'd be in trouble. Seven years prior, I had gone to see a doctor who specialized in bio-identical hormone therapy. He helped me tremendously. It's hard to believe, but I was still suffering the effects of my cancer treatment and early menopause so many years later. I told the oncologist about the hormone pill I was taking. He told me "No problem." He said that the pill went into my bloodstream, while the cream was only topical...

※ ※ ※

...when I found myself being wheeled into the emergency room, I knew he had made a terrible mistake.

My blood pressure was soaring out of control due to an overload of estrogen in my system. No matter what medicine the doctor gave me, my pressure wouldn't go down. I suffered migraine headaches so intense that I was bed ridden for days. I went through a battery of test from blood work to MRI and CT scans, but I kept getting worse. I even went to a holistic doctor to help wean me off the hormone pills. Unfortunately, my pressure kept going up. The doctor kept monitoring me and trying different pressure pills. Nothing worked. Until that day...

※　※　※

...Spirit answered my request. My journey was about to begin. At the time, I would never in my wildest imagination connect what was happening to me to the chapel.

After my last trip to the emergency room, I decided to visit the chapel. I needed peace. I hadn't been there ten minutes, when suddenly, I felt the urge to go to Mass. It was similar to the feeling I had in Florida. I walked out of the chapel. as though in a trance, and drove to church. I had never been to Holy Family Church before, and have no idea how I found it, or how I even got there. It was as though someone else was driving the car.

Mass was over. I saw a priest standing outside talking to some people, and instinctively knew he was from Africa. How I knew that I have no idea. Maybe it's because I love Africa so much and their people? It is truly one of the most beautiful continents on Earth, and the landscape is pure Heaven. I walked over to this unsuspecting young priest and said, "If I build you a chapel will they come?" My inner voice screamed out, "Are you out of your mind?!" Remember, Spirit's voice is never negative. The priest looked at me as though I was crazy. He introduced himself as Father Steven. I asked if he was from Africa. He told me he was from Ghana and only in the states for the summer. Then to my astonishment, I blurted out, "I'll give you ten-thousand dollars if you build a chapel."

I thought I would die. The negative voice kept screaming, "Are you nuts? Where are you getting the money to build a chapel?" Then something funny happened, I started negotiating with myself. Why ten-thousand dollars? Make it five. I couldn't get the number five-thousand out of my mouth. I was in a different state of consciousness. I never ever, even once, thought of doing such a thing. Then I remembered the six little words I said in the chapel. "What can I do for You?"

I never asked Father Steven where in Ghana he was from. I never asked the name of his Parish Church. Nothing! I was ready to hand over ten-thousand dollars to a perfect stranger. God takes care.

The Father told me we couldn't just send money to a foreign country. I had to go through a foundation to make it legal, otherwise, the government would think I was laundering money. Can you imagine? Strangely enough, there just happened to be a Ghana Foundation in Newark, New Jersey. Coincidence? The Foundation gave me papers showing their legitimacy. The thought never entered my mind to ask for anything of that nature, not even for tax purposes, which proved to be invaluable. Spirit was watching over me.

Father Steven and I became good friends. When I told him my goal was to build one-hundred chapels, I thought he would pass out. Sound crazy? Remember, this is Spirit, not me.

One night while watching EWTN, a television network started by Mother Angelica, an amazing nun, who single-handedly built a worldwide television and radio network a panel was discussing the celebration plans for the one hundredth anniversary of the apparitions of Our Lady of Fatima and the miracle of the sun. I fell asleep in the middle of the discussion and woke up thinking I had to build one hundred chapels. When I finally came to my senses I shrugged the idea off as part of a dream. It wasn't that simple. Spirit kept whispering the number one hundred in my ear. After a while, I just gave up. I figured if this is what God wants, it will manifest.

To me, it was no big deal. I thought a hundred chapels would cost around a million dollars. God had given me a writing ability for a reason. Maybe it was for the chapels? All it would take is one hit play or television pilot. That's not unreasonable, right? My writing was already being acknowledged. I just had to be smart enough to take advantage of the opportunities.

I used the money I was saving for Paris to fund the first chapel. My blood pressure was normal by then, and I was off all medication.

Before I gave Father Steven the money I told him I had a few requests. The chapel had to be an Adoration Chapel, open 24/7, and a statue of the Blessed Mother had to be on display. It also had to be dedicated to Our Lady of Fatima. He agreed.

Nothing comes easy, and it took over a year and a half to complete the chapel. You can't just build a chapel. You first have to get permission from the church, and then the resident Bishop. Father Steven handled all the details. My job was to select the statue.

It was May, the month of Mary, and my parish church placed a small statue of the Blessed Mother by the altar. I had never seen such a beautiful statue, her face had the sweetest expression. I wanted it for the chapel in Ghana. I asked Father where I could purchase it. He put me in touch with the lady who donated it. She told me she had bought it in Lewiston, New York, when she went to Our Lady of Fatima Shrine. I went to their online store to order it. There were numerous religious articles and statues of the Blessed Mother. There were several statues of The Blessed Mother that looked similar. I just chose the one with the beautiful smile.

※　※　※

God uses the strangest people. I never put two and two together.

The summer was over, and Father Steven was set to leave for Belgium to complete his studies. He assured me that he would keep in communication with Ghana and check on the progress of the chapel. It took forever to get approval from the higher-ups. Father and I kept in touch via e-mail. We were both so relieved when the chapel was finally completed.

How genius is our God? I realize now, that Spirit gave me the ten-thousand dollar figure because He knew that amount would go far in third world countries.

Father Steven sent me photos of the chapel. My heart leaped for joy when I saw the long line of people waiting outside to get in. The chapel was exactly as I had pictured it.

The Pastor from Ghana added a small stucco structure onto the original church. There are two large windows in the front, beautifully covered in white lace curtains. The chapel has twenty handmade wooden chairs donated by the men of the parish. The floor is white tile. The altar has a magnificent white lace cover that drapes to the floor, handmade by the ladies of the parish. The detail on it is stunning and you can see the love that went into every stitch. On the altar is the main attraction, Jesus in the Holy Eucharist displayed in a beautifully embellished holder of pure silver. To the side of the altar sits a small round table covered in the same lace. On the table is the Lady with the sweet face.

The Letter...

When the letter arrived from the Bishop of Ghana thanking me and my family, I cried. He invited us to the dedication ceremony and closed with...

❋　❋　❋

...Our Lady of Fatima Parish thanks you.

Our Lady of Fatima Parish? I almost fainted, I couldn't believe my eyes! What are the odds? I had no idea when I sent the statue that it was Our Lady of Fatima. I just liked her sweet expression. I never knew that the parish in Ghana was Our Lady of Fatima Parish. How could I? I never asked Father Steven, and he never told me. We were both too busy making plans and dealing with the details.

Isn't it strange that of all the parishes in Ghana, and all the apparitions of God's Mother, I just happened to pick the parish and the statue with the same name? Not a chance! Oh! And only after watching EWTN and hearing of the one hundredth anniversary of Our Lady of Fatima, did I decide to dedicate the chapel in her name. It had to be Spirit's way of letting me know I was on the right track.

Note

Last summer when Father Steven came back to the states, we met at my house for lunch. Joey my musical director/filmmaker and I, decided to make a documentary about the making of a chapel. After lunch, I interviewed Father while Joey filmed us. Father explained how irrational he thought I was when I first approached him. We laughed. Then he proceeded to tell us about the many miraculous healings that had taken place since the opening of the chapel. It didn't surprise me. We had already started to document the miracles surrounding the little chapel at home. We have a young man on tape explaining his healing from pancreatic cancer after frequent visits to the chapel and praying to Saint Jude. He showed us proof by displaying his before and after MRI's. But this was...

Just the Beginning

After Our Lady of Guadalupe healed me, I knew I had to keep my promise and do something special to thank Her. Thus, the *Second Chapel* was born. This time I was on my own and decided to recruit some help.

I met Paul at a fundraiser for abused children. He did a great job in raising money and I thought he'd be a great person to have on my team. I asked him if he would be interested in helping me with the chapels. I told him my story and asked for any assistance he could give me. Paul was intrigued and wanted to learn more. We set up a meeting at my house the following week.

Like clockwork, that following Monday Paul was at my door. He brought his girlfriend, Camille, and his friend, David. I soon found out why they were so interested in helping me, all three are Guardians at the chapel. Coincidence? No. Spirit!

A Guardian is someone who dedicates an hour a week at the chapel to pray and spend time with the Lord. Jesus is never to be left alone. The chapel is open 24/7 for adoration. We do this in memory of the night prior to Jesus's crucifixion. On that night Jesus went to the garden of Gethseman to pray for strength. He sweat blood from the anxiety He suffered, and the knowing of His impending sacrifice. When He came back from His ordeal, He was saddened by the sight of His disciples sleeping.

Matthew 26:40
Then Jesus returned to the disciples and found them sleeping. He said
"Were you not able to keep watch with Me for one hour?" He asked Peter.

❊ ❊ ❊

Paul is a doer. He makes things happen. So, it was perfectly natural for him to come to the meeting prepared. He had a folder full of documents and papers when he arrived. I served coffee and cake as we chatted and got acquainted. Then Paul asked the most logical question "Tell me, how did you build the first chapel? Do you have plans? Did you use an architect? Did you get permission from the Church?" He continued with question, after question, after question.

You can imagine the look of shock on his face when I told him "I didn't do anything. I just gave the money to Father Steven and told him to build me a chapel. And he did."

Everyone looked at me in astonishment. Paul asked, "So how do we start on the next one?" "I have no idea. We just start and let Spirit do the rest." I wasn't trying to be facetious, that's the way I work. I start and learn as I go along, knowing I will be guided. I could see by the look of shock on their faces, that they had second thoughts. Who could blame them? Everyone thought I was delusional, especially when I told them my goal was to build a hundred chapels.

❊ ❊ ❊

I have to give credit to Robert for putting up with me. He never doubted. He always allowed me to be me, with all my quirkiness and irrationalities. I couldn't have done any of this without him.

❊ ❊ ❊

Although bewildered, the chapel team agreed to meet once a week to toss around new ideas. We talked about showing movies to generate funds, but couldn't agree on a film. We talked about raising money using one of my plays. The only problem, my plays are mostly comedies with a slant. I didn't think *Love, Sex and Menopause* would be the appropriate vehicle to raise money for a chapel. After a while, we just gave up. It seemed no matter how hard we tried we couldn't agree on anything.

As I look back now, it seems whenever I tried in the past to put a team together, for whatever reason, it never worked out. I think it's because Jesus wants me to put my faith and trust in Him. It's all about faith!

Paul and I remained friends and kept in touch. God had plans for him, but I wouldn't find that out until much later.

I was going crazy trying to keep my promise to Our Lady of Guadalupe. I couldn't figure out why everyone I contacted regarding the chapel never bothered calling back. Strange. I tried Missions of the Poor, sent letter after letter, to church after church, but not a peep. Who turns down ten-thousand dollars?

I started using the money I put aside, until little by little it was all gone. God knew I would drain my bank account before I broke a promise to Him. I prayed for an answer. It came in the form of a phone call.

Mrs. Gillman was on the phone. I had no desire to work as a designer after God put writing into my heart. That is, until the morning of the call. I had designed her entire house several years prior, but she was looking to change her master bedroom into an en-suite and she needed my help. I hesitated at first. Then Spirit whispered "Take the job." I made exactly ten-thousand dollars. When Spirit wants something done, He provides.

Meanwhile, now that I had the money, I still couldn't get anyone interested in building a chapel. After almost two years of trying and getting nowhere, I finally gave up. I said to Our Lady, "I tried everything. When you're ready, and if it's your desire, I trust you will let me know. I leave everything in your hands."

A few weeks later, Paul contacted me. He asked if I was still interested in building another chapel. I guess he thought it was a passing phase, "Of course," I answered. He told me about his friend Father Youssef who works with abandoned children in Honduras. Paul said Father told him he was serving Mass on an old kitchen table, and how he wished he had a chapel. That's when Paul thought of me. He gave me Father's e-mail if I wanted to follow up.

The Miracle

I immediately sent Father an e-mail telling him I would be honored to fund a chapel if he adhered to my request: there had to be Adoration, it had to be completed for ten-thousand dollars, and it must be dedicated to Our Lady of Guadalupe.

The following week I received a call from Honduras. It was Father Youssef. He said he cried when he received my e-mail. He told me no one knew, not even Paul, that he had been praying to Our Lady of Guadalupe for a chapel. My eyes filled with tears. God, in His perfect timing, brought us together for His glory. Our Lady was waiting for Father Youssef.

The money went through the Franciscan Friars of the Renewal in New York. Father worked there before moving to Honduras to serve the poor.

I was overwhelmed with excitement. The chapel for Our Lady was about to begin. Father's nephew, an architect, drew up the plans for free. Everything was going fine until...

❈ ❈ ❈

...darkness reared its ugly head.

The Bishop from the area refused to give Father his permission to build a chapel. He was afraid it might be a conflict of interest with the Honduras government.

Father labored hard to get permission to use the land where the chapel would be built. He pleaded with the authorities. He told them how important the chapel was for the children and the community. He did everything in his power to convince them. Unfortunately, the answer was always the same.

Father was heartbroken and defeated. He prayed to Our Lady. But then, just an hour before he was due to call me with the bad news, the Bishop called with the approval.

The chapel's design is simple concrete block. This kind of structure protects the people from the rain and the extreme heat of the region. There is no means of air conditioning in this impoverished section of Honduras.

The interior of the chapel consists of twenty-five wooden pews which adorn each side of the center aisle, a simple handmade wooden altar that sits on an elevated platform above which hangs a large wooden cross. To the side of the altar is a large portrait of Our Lady of Guadalupe. The simplicity of the chapel is powerful.

In gratitude, the men of the community hand-carved a wooden sign to place over the door. It read, 'Our Lady of Guadalupe Chapel.'

The Choice Is Never Mine

I never choose where, or for who, a chapel is destined to go. God chooses. Chapel THREE came as a complete surprise. It manifested on the day of my brother's memorial.

※　※　※

I was late in planning Michael's service. I wanted a specific day September 19, the day of his birthday, impossible to get unless booked in advance. I called the rectory, and sure enough, it was already reserved. I was just about to call another church when my cell phone rang. It was the receptionist from the rectory calling back to tell me they just received a cancellation. Funny how things suddenly work out when Spirit is involved.

The day before the service, I received notice that Father John, the priest I requested for the ceremony, was suddenly called out of town and that Father Mendez would be taking his place. I wasn't happy. I wanted Father John, but God had other plans. I didn't know Father Mendez and was anxious to meet him. I called the next day and requested a meeting for late afternoon to go over the details of the memorial. He accepted.

When Father Mendez opened the rectory door and greeted me with a big smile, I immediately felt at ease. I explained to him that I wanted the Memorial Mass dedicated to Divine Mercy. I explained the strange circumstances surrounding my brother's death. He asked me to tell him about my brother. He said that he wanted to get to know him. He wasn't just doing his job, he was sincerely interested. I was touched by his thoughtfulness.

We talked about my brother and I asked about his family. He told me that he comes from Sri Lanka. His face lit with joy as he related stories about his beautiful country and his wonderful family. At that moment, we became friends. As I was about to leave, I asked him where I could buy Divine Mercy cards. I wanted to give them out at the ceremony. "Don't spend the money. I have some right here," he said. He opened the desk drawer and pulled out a stack of beautifully laminated Divine Mercy cards. I enclosed the prayer card with a letter recalling what happened to Michael on the day he died and gave it to all the guests. I wanted everyone to know how God's mercy and love saved my beloved brother.

The service was beautiful. I spoke to the organist earlier that day and selected the music. I told him I wanted lively songs, not a death march. I ordered a beautiful basket of white flowers for the altar, and arranged a luncheon for my guests. I wanted everything to be perfect. My brother was cremated in Florida, but he received the ceremony he deserved.

After the Mass I grabbed Suzanne and her husband Jeffrey, and told Father to bless them. He did. Jennifer had already left the church. I was almost out the door when I realized I had forgotten to thank Father for giving such a beautiful and heartwarming eulogy. As I was walking towards him, I heard Spirit say, "Build him a chapel." I looked Father Mendez straight in the eye and said, "Thank you for a such a beautiful ceremony. Oh, and by the way, I'm going to build you a chapel."

Chapel Three The Miracle

It was a warm sunny morning when I met Father Mendez to discuss the chapel. The sun shined brightly through the stained glass window, washing his office with rays of translucent color. As I sat there admiring the light, Father entered and greeted me with a big smile.

I told Father the story about the day I sat in the little chapel and asked Jesus, "What can I do for You." And how Spirit put in my heart the day of the memorial, to build a chapel for him. He sat there with a big grin on his face. I was about to begin my next sentence when he stopped me. "Wait! I have something to show you." He rushed out of the room. Two minutes later he was back with a blueprint under his arm. He placed it on the desk and rolled it out. "Look! This is the church I was building in Sri Lanka when I was called to come to the states. It's dedicated to the Sacred Heart of Jesus."

There it was, the validation. Memories of my childhood flashed before me. I was back in Brooklyn watching my mother run in the pouring rain to catch her bus for work. I saw myself sitting in front of the window crying. I was praying to a picture of the Sacred Heart...

✳   ✳   ✳

...Father's voice brought my attention back to the blueprint on his desk. He opened his desk drawer and took out a batch of pictures and showed me the ground breaking ceremony for the new church. I told Father, "I'm sorry Father I'm not interested in making a donation to the church. I'm here to build a chapel, and it has to be completed for ten-thousand dollars." He smiled and told me to take a closer look at the drawing. He stretched the paper so I could get a better look. On closer examination, I saw on either side of the main church, there were two small structures. Father explained that one is for the saints, and the other is for adoration. We hugged. He told me he would start the Adoration Chapel first. He said ten-thousand US dollars equals one million four hundred and eighty-five thousand Sri Lanka rupees, enough to finish that part of the building.

Father would be visiting his family in July and told me he would personally supervise the project. In the meantime, he would instruct his friend in Sri Lanka, to get started on the work. He wanted to get as much done as possible before the rainy season.

It was late August when Father arrived back in the states. He was excited to show me the progress they had made on the chapel. I was overjoyed. The roof was on, and construction was moving along on the interior. We celebrated with coffee and donuts.

❊ ❊ ❊

This wasn't Father's first attempt at building a church. He had raised money in the past to construct two other churches in the region. Whenever a church was needed, they went to Father Mendez. The last one he built was in honor of Saint Anthony. My beloved Saint. Then he shared something extraordinary with me. He told me that during the building of Saint Anthony's Church he experienced his own miracle.

I was intrigued, as I listened to Father tell the story. He explained how he watched as the workers finished the remaining details on the church. As they began to pack and get ready to leave, Father panicked, as he realized he didn't have enough money to pay them. They finished before schedule, and Father was frantic. He knew he was almost thirty thousand dollars short. He went to his room and prayed silently to Saint Anthony not to make him look bad because the men trusted him. As the men waited to be paid, Father received a call. It was from a donor. Father told the man about his dilemma. The man told him not to worry and that he would transfer money to his account. The generous donor not only sent father enough money to pay the workers, but also an extra twenty-thousand dollars for whatever else he needed. Saint Anthony came through. Pray to him.

❊ ❊ ❊

The chapel in Sri Lanka is different from the other two chapels because it's connected to a brand new church. At present, it is still under construction. But a hand-carved wooden statue of the Blessed Mother will be placed in the new chapel dedicated to the Sacred Heart.

Past Experiences

Building the chapels are not the first time Spirit used me to do something for Him. Another time, He used me to help two impoverished children in India. It all started one cold March morning when...

※ ※ ※

...I woke up shivering. I jumped out of bed to get another blanket when I heard Spirit whisper the name Saint Joseph in my ear. I brushed it off and went back to bed. All throughout the day I kept hearing the saint's name. When Spirit wants something done He can be relentless.

I was working with Crossroads at the time. So, in my mind, the logical explanation was to make a donation to the organization if they allowed me to put a statue of Saint Joseph on the premises. I went to them with the offer but they refused. The administrator told me it was against state rules to put anything religious on their grounds. After that, I did what I should have done in the first place. I waited.

A few weeks later at Mass, I heard Father George speaking. He was visiting from another parish to solicit money for children in his native India. After Mass he was outside Church with pictures of the children. He said it would cost twenty-five dollars a month for each child to go to school. I felt bad no one was paying much attention to him, so I decided to help. I gave Father a check and my address. It was impossible for me to choose from all the adorable children he showed me, so I told him to pick two and send me the details.

I never gave it much thought after that, until I received the letter...

On the letterhead was the name of Father's Parish: Saint Joseph's Parish Albany, New York.

※ ※ ※

That was six years ago. The children are now entering high school. They write to me, send pictures, and keep me posted on progress reports from school. Father and I remain good friends until today.

※ ※ ※

Other Strange Coincidences

My heart was heavy. I feared for my grandchildren, for all children. I thought about the world they were forced to grow up in, and I prayed. As I recited my morning gratitude, I heard Spirit say, "Pray to Mary." I started to pray to the Blessed Mother when suddenly I got this bright idea. I thought how much more effective would it be if the entire world prayed to her?

The next day, I was on my computer drafting a letter. I explained the plight of our children in today's society, and emphasized the importance of saying one Hail Mary at every Mass. I printed the letter and made copies.

I literally hand-delivered each letter to every church I could find. I traveled to several boroughs before I ran out of steam. Exhausted from a hard day's work, I flopped into my favorite chair and put my feet up. Then I heard Spirit say, "Why didn't you use e-mail?"

God uses the weak and the foolish. I certainly fit the bill. I laughed at my own stupidity. After a greatly needed cup of coffee, I e-mailed the letter to every Catholic Church in the United States and beyond. A daunting task to say the least.

Next on my agenda was to contact Cardinal Dolan. I sent a special letter detailing my concern for our children, and how much they needed the Blessed Mother's guidance. I pleaded for one Hail Mary at every Mass. I signed it, 'A Concerned Grandmother.'

How presumptuous of me. In my naivete I thought the letter would be received with open arms. I was wrong. Cardinal Dolan did write back. He was kind and understanding, but in essence told me he couldn't do anything. That in order to change or add anything during the Holy Mass he would need special permission from the Pope. I was devastated and decided to give up. A few months later it happened...

❅ ❅ ❅

...we were having lunch when Robert suddenly jumped up from the table and announced that we were going to church. I told him to go by himself as I wasn't in the mood. He insisted we go together. I reluctantly agreed just to shut him up. He was relentless.

When we walked into the lobby of the church, I could hear a woman's voice over the speaker praying... "Hail Mary, full of grace..."

❄ ❄ ❄

...Naturally it caught my attention. As I opened the door, I saw a young lady at the pulpit reciting the rosary. I thought that was strange. People were coming in for Mass. What in the world was she doing? After Mass, I approached her to find out what was going on. To my amazement, she told me that the Pastor instructed her to say a rosary as the people entered for Mass. He told her "Let them pray for our children, instead of gossiping."

I smiled as I heard Spirit say, "You asked for a Hail Mary, I gave you a rosary." That was four years ago. The rosary is still being said before the 5 o'clock Mass on Saturday, and before the 12 o'clock Mass on Sunday. Miracle? Coincidence? You be the judge.

The Latest Miracle

My story wouldn't be complete, without telling you about my beloved Saint Anthony. He is always depicted holding the infant Jesus.

My daughter Jennifer was in trouble. She hadn't worked in a while due to her battle with breast cancer and her weakened immune system from celiac disease. She needed help so I prayed to Saint Anthony for Jennifer's healing and a job. I had never prayed to him before, but after hearing Father Mendez's story, I decided to ask for his help.

Then I took a leap of faith...

❄ ❄ ❄

...I told Jennifer not to lose heart, and that Saint Anthony would come to her aid. I told her in a few months she would land a HUGE job. I kept stressing the word huge. I wanted to lift her spirits.

A month had passed and nothing. We were coming down to the wire. I began to panic. I figured maybe Saint Anthony need a push. I didn't want him to look bad to Jennifer. Can you imagine, I was worried about Saint Anthony?

I went to church and stood at the foot of the Saint Anthony and the Baby Jesus statue and said, "Baby Jesus, please don't make Saint Anthony look bad. I promised my daughter he would help her."

In truth, I was losing faith. I was like a little kid standing in front of that statue. A kid who received an immediate response.

I was driving home from church when Jen called. She sounded so excited. She told me how she landed a huge job on a television show, and a reoccurring part on another. Her career was back in full bloom. More importantly, her test for the BRCA Gene came back negative. I was sobbing so hard I had to pull over. I was in awe of the supernatural power of faith, combined with a mother's love. Once again my prayers were answered. This time it was through Saint Anthony and the Baby Jesus.

❋ ❋ ❋

I know this all must sound crazy to you. It sounds crazy to me too, but I'm telling you the truth. I want you to know and have faith that miracles can and do happen. I'm living proof!

The only reason I'm opening up and telling you this is to give you hope. I'm no one special. I'm not holy or at church every minute of the day. I truly believe the only reason these things happen to me, is because I totally BELIEVE they will! I believe beyond a shadow of a doubt, that what I ask for will be given to me. And it always is! It will for you too. You just have to believe it will.

Matthew 7:9-11
"Which of you, if your son asks for bread, will give him a stone? Or if he asks for a fish, will give him a snake? If you, then, though you are evil, know how to give good gifts to your children, how much more will your Father in heaven give good gifts to those who ask him!"

****** Food For Thought ******

Know that you can communicate with God. He is not someone out there. He is here, with us, in us. I want you to experience His presence just like I did that day in church, when he surrounded me with His love. I want you to know that feeling of joy, of exhilaration. Jesus said, ask and you shall receive. Seek and you shall find. Seek Him!

Hebrews 11:6
"And without faith it is impossible to please God, because anyone who comes to him must believe that he exists and that he rewards those who earnestly seek him."

Jesus knows when He calls, I listen. I learned as a child to trust Him. I live my life that way. Learn to listen for Spirit. Never allow negative or fearful thoughts to enter your mind or heart. Go out on a limb! Take chances.

I've planned trips to exotic places, put on plays, built chapels, all on faith. Live adventurously, trusting that Spirit will guide you. Never let the fear of not having enough stop you from doing anything. If I put money first, I would never have traveled the world, or done anything else for that matter. First the dream, then the way. If it's Spirit-led it will always work out.

I'm not suggesting not to be sensible. A good rule to follow is: Give, save, and spend. Don't put things off. Some people save all their lives and never do anything because they live in fear and what if's? They live for tomorrow. Wrong! There is no promise of tomorrow. We only assume there will be.

Give to others in love and knowing that God will reward you generously. Spend money on the things you enjoy. Don't try and compete with others. Let them compete with you. Save for a rainy day. Then step out of the boat! It's a phrase I refer to often.

Jesus Walks on Water

"Lord, if it's you," Peter replied, "tell me to come to you on the water."

"Come He said."
Then Peter got down out of the boat, walked on the water and came toward Jesus. When he saw the wind, he was afraid and, beginning to sink, cried out, "Lord, save me!"
Immediately Jesus reached out his hand and caught him. "You of little faith," he said, "why did you doubt?"

"For truly I tell you, if you have faith the size of a mustard seed, you can say to this mountain, "move from here to there,' and it will move. Nothing will be impossible for you."

❋　❋　❋

Jesus is all about Faith. Before I do anything, I say to Him. "Lord I'm stepping out of the boat. You have to help me." Most of the time I'm praying "Jesus, I'm out of the boat and sinking. Jesus I'm up to my nose in water. Help!"

Only God knows where I go from here.
Three chapels down, 97 to go...

PART 2

Prayer and Visualization

13

Something More

I'M SURE YOU'VE asked yourself a thousand times, "What are we doing here? What's it all about? Are we here for a moment in time, only to die and that's it? What's the point? Why bother striving for a dream only to have it taken away in the end? There has to be something more." I'm here to tell you, based on my experiences, that there is.

Let's backtrack a little. Imagine it's the year before your conception. Where are you? Are you floating around in space somewhere? Maybe you're playing with the dinosaurs, or are you an egg, or a sperm, looking for a place to settle? Better yet, imagine you've landed.

You're now a fetus, attached to an umbilical cord, inside your mother's womb, and you have to make your way to Earth via a narrow birth canal that resembles a tunnel, with a light at the end.

It's hard to imagine ourselves taking the journey of birth, or being a helpless child, yet we all have. Then why do we fear death so much? Isn't it pretty much the same thing? The only difference is, we can't go out the way we came in, and, we don't know the outcome. Or do we?

We are in the consciousness that we have always been here, and that death is for the other guy. We fight to stay young, look young, be young. All in a futile attempt to cheat death. We're afraid to go back into the unknown, even though we have already experienced it before birth.

What if something wonderful awaits us? What if we find ourselves in an amazing place? A place of happiness and joy? A place called Heaven?

People who have had near-death experiences, all seem to say the same thing. That at the moment of death, they leave their body and go through a tunnel. They also say they're surrounded by a white light. They see dead relatives, and feel a loving presence.

John 3:16
"For God so loved the world that he gave his one and only Son, that whoever believes in him shall not perish but have eternal life."

John 14:1
Jesus said, "I am the resurrection and the life. The one who believes in me will live, even though they die;

Losing someone you love is never easy, knowing they never leave you will give you comfort. When you feel sad, confused, and grief-stricken, meditate on these words:

Lord, Father, I know my loved one, is in Your hands and surrounded by Your love.

Help me to find peace, in knowing they are with You, safe and free from pain.

Console me in my time of sorrow.

Help me to see the light. To feel their touch and know they are still with me.

Help me to know that I will be reunited with them someday. And that they continue to watch over me and my family.

Heal my pain.

Visualization from Fear:

This exercise is designed to take away the trepidation of the unknown.

(Record this message, so you can listen to it each day)

Shut the curtains and close the lights, then put on music that simulates the sound of the ocean. Now, lie down and put a warm cloth over your eyes. Light a candle that smells of seagrass, or place a bowl of steaming sea salt water next to you. Take a few minutes to relax. Now, breathe. Feel the sound of the ocean washing over you. Feel yourself floating on top of it. Feel peaceful and light as you and the ocean become one. Slowly picture yourself as a tiny speck, an embryo, inside a bubble. Feel safe and warm as you float around in the fluid that engulfs you. Watch as your body starts to form. See your eyes, nose, ears, and mouth begin to take shape. Picture yourself as a perfect little being. Admire every tiny detail, from you pinkie finger, down to your tiny toe. See yourself growing bigger with every breath, until you are ready to be born.

While you are floating around, do you hear anything? Your mother's voice? Music? Do you feel love, a touch? Anything? Feel the excitement as you get ready to make you way to Earth. See the light. Feel loving hands grab you, as you leave your warm safe cocoon. Breathe in the warmth.

Feel yourself being placed on your mother. Feel her touch, her kiss, hear her soft voice. Feel safe and content.

Breathe in the love...

※ ※ ※

...Now see yourself back on the ocean. See yourself floating. You are one with the ocean again. Feel the waves, the soft breeze on your face. The sun shinning down on you. Breathe in the smell of the sea. Relax and let the ocean cradle you. Breathe. This time see Heaven. Feel yourself floating. See your body transformed into a sparkling translucent light. Feel the weightlessness, feel the overwhelming sense of joy. See the sky, mountains, streams, and rivers. Visualize a rainbow, a magnificent canvas of colors, so bright it hurts your eyes. See a beautiful mosaic of babies laughing, and playing, as they run through a field of bright yellow daisies. Feel the Light. In the far distance, see the animals coexisting and commingling with each other and you. Pick up a baby tiger. Feel it, play with it, caress it. Breathe in the colors. Feel the brilliant white light, as it wraps you in a blanket of unconditional love. Breathe in the love. Now slowly see yourself back on the ocean floating.

Revelation Chapter 21 (a look at heaven)
The twelve gates [were] twelve pearls; every several gate was of one pearl: and the street of the city [was] pure gold, as it were transparent glass.

Whenever fear arises, close your eyes and go back in time and experience the miracle of your birth, and the promise of Heaven. It will give you strength and a sense of peace, and hope.

Simple prayer: Father, thank You for giving me eternal life. Thank You, for this chance to know, love, and serve You.

Note: Jesus died so we can be with him in paradise.

14

That Empty Place

I KNOW WHAT it's like to feel lost, lonely, and discouraged. I've been there many times myself. We start out full of hopes and dreams, then something happens, or we take a wrong turn and suddenly, we're on the sideline watching our dreams dissipate into thin air.

We convince ourselves that everything is fine, that we can handle it, when deep down inside there's a nagging pain that won't go away. It sneaks up on us when we're quiet, still, and alone with our thoughts.

It could be a relationship, a troubled marriage, sickness, or the loss of a loved one. It could be a host of things that throws us off track: losing a job, or working at one we hate, can be earth-shattering. From money problems, to aging parents, it's something we all face sooner or later. It's called life, which at times can be devastating. What can we do when trouble strikes? We can give it over to a Higher Power, the same power that created the Universe and us.

The Universe

We hear the term Universe used all the time. Phrases like, "Give it to the Universe. Leave it to the Universe. Put it out into the Universe." What does that mean? Are we seeking guidance from the stars, the moon, Pluto? Why are we so afraid to use the term God?

Scientists say that the Universe was created by a big bang. If that's true, then someone had to set off the explosion? It had to be a power so great, so awesome, so all-encompassing that it boggles the mind.

According to Genesis I: In the beginning, God created the heavens and the earth. Think of a power so unimaginable and yet, open and available to us. How do we connect with this power? Simple. We just ask to.

Connecting with the Divine

The easiest way to connect with the Divine is through Gratitude.

Psalm 118:24
This is the day which the LORD has made; Let us rejoice and be glad in it.

Every day, as soon as you wake up, take a few minutes to count your blessings. No matter what kind of mood you're in when you open your eyes, do it! If you can't think of anything to be thankful for, fake it. Start off by saying:

Thank You, Lord, for another day.
Thank You, I'm here to see it.
(Repeat these words over and over until you hear them in your sleep.)

Each day, add another blessing. If you're a runner or go to the gym, give thanks while exercising. Giving thanks is a form of meditation, which provides a sense of well-being and makes you forget your troubles.

Think about all that is good in your life. If you are outside in nature, take in your surroundings. Give thanks for the wonder. Notice the sound of the birds, wind, the ocean, or the rain drops. Take note of the trees, flowers, the sun, or the snow...

❊ ❊ ❊

...the point is to just TAKE NOTICE and give thanks! After your morning shower, look at yourself in the mirror and be grateful. Learn to love and accept yourself as you are now, a living, breathing, miracle; one of a kind, unique, and made in the image of Almighty God.

I promise you, if you continually practice gratitude every day, and not let your mind take control of your thoughts, your day will go much better. You will feel better and handle things more efficiently. Your circumstances may remain the same, but your attitude towards them will change and make it easier to cope. Changing what you think from the minute you wake up is essential for your well-being.

Be diligent! It's difficult to break bad habits. Most of us wake up with a To-Do-List on our minds. We never stop to think of God or Divine love. We only think of Him when we are desperate. Practice this simple task of Gratitude each morning, until it becomes a habit. I guarantee if you do, you will not only lower your blood pressure, but improve your overall health and change your life for the better.

Establish a Relationship

Matthew 6:33
Your Heavenly Father knows what you need. Seek first the kingdom of God and His righteousness, and all these things will be added unto you.

If you are trying to establish a relationship with someone, what would you do? Would you ignore them, or go out of your way to get to know them better, or perhaps spend some quality time with them? The same is true for God. If you want to have a relationship with the Divine, you must spend time with Him.

Instead of talking to friends or co-workers about your troubles, try quieting your mind each day by connecting to His Divine presence. Ask to know Him better by saying:

Father, help me to connect with Your love.
Help me to feel Your Presence.
Help me get closer to You.
Help me to know You better.

Visualization to Connect with the Divine

Visualization is an important tool. Use it to bring yourself closer to God, to feel Him, to be with Him. I want you to feel the ecstasy, happiness, and bliss I felt that day in church when He engulfed me in His love.

Visualization

(Record this message, so you can listen to it each day)

Find a quiet place. Close your eyes. Breathe. Visualize a white Light. See the Light entering your body from the top of your head. Breathe in the Light. Imagine the Light as a waterfall washing gently over your entire body. Breathe. See the image of Jesus as He approaches you. Visualize Him standing there. Visualize His face. Feel Him. Picture His loving arms reaching out to you. Imagine yourself as a wounded sparrow. See Him picking you up. See Him holding you in His hands. Feel His love surrounding and protecting you. Breathe. With each breath, breathe in His love. His mercy. His power. Now with your mind, talk to Him. Not with words, But with thoughts. See the sparrow basking in His warmth. Feel it. Let it nurture you. Breathe.

Keep practicing visualization. Don't worry if you can't picture Jesus. Just envision an image with out-stretched hands. Don't be discouraged if your thoughts and worries distract you. When that happens, take a deep breath and see the sparrow. Focus on the sparrow. See it being healed, loved, caressed.

Gratitude and visualization are great tools; and prayer is another.

Prayer

Prayer is nothing more than conversation with God. Jesus prayed all the time. He drew strength from His heavenly Father through prayer. The most important part of prayer is to be sincere. Don't speak empty words. Speak with your heart. Tell the Lord what is on your mind. Talk to Him like you would talk to a friend. Use His words.

Luke 11:1
One day in a place where Jesus had just finished praying, one of His disciples requested, "Lord, teach us to pray, just as John taught his disciples." Jesus told them, "When you pray, say:

"Our Father, Who art in heaven
Hallowed be Thy Name;
Thy kingdom come,
Thy will be done,
on earth as it is in heaven.
Give us this day our daily bread,
and forgive us our trespasses,
as we forgive those who trespass against us;
and lead us not into temptation,
but deliver us from evil.

Expectation

Jeremiah 33:3
Call to me and I will answer you and will tell you great and hidden things that you have not known.

When you pray to God, pray with EXPECTATION. Faith is the most important part of prayer. Most of us pray but never expect our prayers to be answered; we hope they will be and we half believe. You must speak it as if it were so!

When you go to God with your problems, thank Him for answering your prayers. Remember, you are not talking to someone in the clouds or someone who is unapproachable. You are talking to your Heavenly Father who resides in you. We are all His children. He created each and every one of us. He cares. He wants to see us happy.

John 15:5
I am the vine, and you are the branches. The one who remains in Me, and I in him, will bear much fruit. For apart from Me you can do nothing.

Every day thank Him for His blessings. If you are in a troubled relationship for example, ask Jesus to intervene. Instead of speaking about how bad things are, speak blessings over the relationship, talk about how things are getting better, even if you don't see it. Envision it! Believe it will happen!

I'm not telling you not to address the issues. I'm only asking that you have faith in His Divine love. He will guide and show you the way.

Your words are very important! What you speak and think about all day long, will manifest into your life. If you only speak negative words over a situation, then negative things will occur. The same goes for positivity. Know the power of your words! If you want to manifest good and fruitful relationships, you must speak positive words over them.

Ephesians 4:29
Let no corrupting talk come out of your mouths, but only such as is good for building up, as fits the occasion, that it may give grace to those who hear.

Philippians 4:6
Be anxious for nothing, but in everything, by prayer and petition, with thanksgiving, present your requests to God.

Simple prayer: Father, I give all my cares and worries to You. Thank You for taking care of them for me. Jesus, I trust in You.

Note: Only He can fill that space. He does, and He will.

15

The Healing Power
of God's Love

Hebrews 11:1
Now faith is the assurance of what we hope for and the certainty of what we do not see.

Romans 8:24
For in this hope we were saved; but hope that is seen is no hope at all. Who hopes for what he can already see?

Corinthians 4:18
So we fix our eyes not on what is seen, but on what is unseen. For what is seen is temporary, but what is unseen is eternal.

Faith

What is Jesus telling us? He is telling us to believe in Him. Faith is the most important part of the equation. Without it, Jesus says we can do nothing, and with it, we can move mountains.

Mark 11:23
Truly I tell you that if anyone says to this mountain, 'Be lifted up and thrown into the sea,' and has no doubt in his heart but believes that it will happen, it will be done for him.

Healing

In order to heal yourself of a physical or emotional illness, you must first believe that you can. Then take steps to help in that healing.

Believe in His Love

If a doctor gives you a bad prognosis, listen, but refuse to accept the outcome. Believe in a Higher Power and His love. When the doctor told me I had advanced cancer, the first thing that popped into my head was, "He's crazy! I have no intention of leaving my children. I refuse to be sick!"

A doctor has an obligation to tell you the facts. The test results, the outcome according to his charts and survival rates. Your obligation is not to accept it. No one has the right to tell you how much time you have left or do not have. Only God knows the day and the hour. When you hear the shocking news, and someone telling you, "Better get your things in order," what happens to your emotions? You feel hopeless, depressed, and anxious. Your mind starts spinning out of control. You feel dizzy. Your negative emotions take over and compromise your immune system just when you need it the most. Your heart goes into overtime beating out of control. These feelings put your body immediately in a downward spiral.

Listen halfheartedly. Take time to think things through. Pray on it. Visualize. Research your options. Whether you chose conventional treatment or alternative medicine, make sure you're at peace with yourself. Don't let fear guide your decision. Ask Spirit to help you. Know that you're not alone in your battle. You have the power of Almighty God within you and with you. If God can make the sun, He can heal you. Never forget that. I'm living proof... now it's up to you to do your part. It's your responsibility to take action in helping yourself to wellness through God's love.

The Power of Intention

The power of intention is imperative! God's desire is for you to have a healthy body, mind, and spirit. You belong to Him. He will never leave or forsake you.

John 1:2
Beloved, I pray that all may go well with you and that you may be in good health, as it goes well with your soul.

Psalm 147:3 *He heals the brokenhearted and binds up their wounds.*

Proverbs 17:22
A joyful heart is good medicine, but a crushed spirit dries up the bones.

You will never heal yourself if you don't first intend to. You must beyond a shadow of a doubt intend to heal. You must believe that you will be healed. Every day say to yourself with conviction:

I trust in God's healing power.
I am healthy, strong, and resilient.
I will overcome.
I have a healthy immune system.
My body will do as I tell it to do.
I have no intention of being ill.

I will flourish and see a long healthy life.
My body, mind, soul, and spirit, are strong and will overcome.
His Divine Love and power live within me.
I get stronger and stronger every day.
I give praise and thanksgiving for my healthy body.
Jesus, I trust in You. Thank You for making me whole.

Visualization for Healing

Before you start, give praise and thanksgiving for your healing. When scary thoughts arise, immediately, declare power over them. When you do your Visualization (which you MUST) focus on the Light.

Start by...

...getting in a comfortable position. Play soft inspirational music, light a lavender-scented candle, dim the lights, then take a few minutes to relax your mind and body. Now breathe, taking the time to follow the breath as it travels through your body.

Now picture a bright Light. See the image of out-stretched Hands, surrounded by the Light. Breathe in the Light. See the hands cupping the Light and pouring it over you. See the Light move over your body, and on to the affected area.

If you have a tumor, see the Light going through it, breaking it into tiny pieces, and dissolving it into the Light. Breathe.

Now, picture the Light as an army of soldiers surrounding and destroying all the bad cells in your body.

※　※　※

See the loving hands of light drawing closer to you.
Feel the healing.
Feel it. Know it. Believe it!
See the sparrow. Feel the mighty hands of God healing its wing. You are the sparrow.

Feel the healing power of God's love and claim it.
Breathe it in, as you bask in the warmth of His safety.
Feel the joy of His unconditional love and give thanks.

(Repeat this visualization twice a day for 20 minutes).

When I was going through my cancer treatments, I had an excellent doctor. Doctor Gonzalez, my radiologist, taught me the power of visualization. It works! Do it!

Sleep

I can't say enough about sleep and its importance. Sleep is when your body heals and replenishes itself. It strengthens your immune system. Sleep is one of the most important parts of the healing process.

When I was fighting cancer and raising two small children, I worked my sleep/naps around them. When they rested, so did I. I went to bed as early as possible. When you're not feeling well, all you want to do is sleep anyway. Don't wait until something happens to develop the habit of getting a good night's sleep.

Make sure you take the time to unwind before getting into bed. A warm calming bath with lavender or bath salts will increase relaxation, relieve muscle pain, and decrease stress.

Make your room conducive for sleeping. Shut off the television and your phone. Remove the laptop, iPad and anything electronic, and darken your room. When you're fighting an illness, be it a life threatening disease or the flu, you need to rest. Try to get at least eight to ten hours of sleep a night. Take an afternoon nap if possible.

Laughter

Believe it or not, laughter is found to be good for your health. It makes sense. When you're laughing, you're not stressing. Laughter relieves tension and strengthens the immune system. The great Norman

Cousins, a professor of Medicine at the University of California, used laughter and humor to heal himself from a life-threatening illness in the early 1960. It was documented in his book and movie, *Anatomy of an Illness*. He is the pioneer of his time. You can watch his story of recovery on YouTube. It's also worth the effort to read his book.

Norman Cousins believed that if negative emotions can make you sick, then the opposite must be true. He proved his concept by recovering from his illness by using laughter, taking massive doses of Vitamin C, eating organic food, and doing moderate exercise.

Exercise

No matter how bad you are feeling, you must exercise. Walk around the room if that's the only thing you can do. Try sitting in a chair and doing yoga. Exercise is movement. It improves health and gives you peace of mind.

Food

Drinking lots of water is imperative. Make green drinks of kale, spinach, broccoli, cucumber, celery, spirulina, lemon, and ginger. You can find cold-pressed drinks in most health food stores. Beet and carrot juice combined with the greens are a powerful combination. It's true, chicken soup is still good for you. Bone broth is another great alternative. Vitamin C is a biggie. There is a powdered form of the vitamin you can buy. Take it every day. Green tea is also great. Stay away from sugar!

Make sure to check with your doctor before starting any exercise or vitamin program.

Matthew 18:20
Jesus said, "For where two or three gather in my name, there am I with them."

Ask friends and family to pray with you for healing. Put your name on the prayer list at your local church. Attend Healing Masses. Call a prayer hotline and ask them to pray with you for healing. Quote the following scriptures every day:

Isaiah 41:10
Fear not, for I am with you; be not dismayed, for I am your God; I will strengthen you, I will help you, I will uphold you with my righteous right hand.

Jeremiah 33:6
Behold, I will bring to it health and healing, and I will heal them and reveal to them abundance of prosperity and security.

Psalm 41:3
The Lord sustains him on his sickbed; in his illness, you restore him to full health.

Simple Prayer: Father, thank You for healing me. Thank You for giving me strength. Thank You for the many healthy years that You have bestowed on me, and continue to bestow on me. Jesus I trust in You.

Note: God loves you, and desires to give you good health.

16

A Practical Guide to Living Your Dream

WE HAVE ALL heard the term "change your life." I think "improve your life" is a much better phrase. Why put all that pressure on yourself to be something you're not? Learn to accept yourself unconditionally. It's the first step in realizing your individual potential. Why make yourself crazy? Take time to praise yourself with the realization that there is no one exactly like you in the entire Universe. You are one of a kind. You can do anything you want if you believe you can. Once you've accepted yourself, you can go from there. Don't waste precious time thinking that your life is miserable, when the truth is, you're unhappy with the circumstances you find yourself in at this time.

Stop comparing yourself or your life to others. Most people are probably dealing with the same issues as you are. Don't be fooled into thinking what you see on the outside is a reflection of what's going on inside of someone. Most people walk around with masks on. They hide their true feelings from themselves and others. Wasting time complaining about your current situation, only puts your dreams on hold.

Dream

Everything starts with a vision, thought, or desire. Think of a small child and the wonder they experience when they see something they want. What's the first thing the child does? They reach out and grab it. If someone takes it away, the child screams and hollers until they get it back. A child has no filter. They do whatever it takes to get what they want. That is until the word NO is pounded into their little heads.

Don't let your past dictate you present. I'm sure somewhere along the line you heard the word NO. You heard it so many times that you forgot how to dream. You did what you were told to do. What everyone expected, not what you really wanted.

Your need to make a living, forced you in a direction you never intended to go. Fear of not being accepted, loved, understood, or wanted, might have put you on the same path, so if you're unhappy, it's time to revisit those dreams.

It's Never Too Late

Don't be fooled into thinking, you're too old, too late, or you don't have the right qualifications. Stop making excuses and start making changes.

Kentucky Fried Chicken was founded by Harland Sanders when he was 65 and out of work. J.K. Rowling was unemployed, divorced, and a single mother when she started writing *Harry Potter*. She was also dealing with depression from the loss of her mother, yet, she kept on writing. She held on to her dream and went from welfare to a millionaire in only five short years. Dreams do come true! Dream BIG!

Know Your Purpose

Everyone has a purpose. We're not here just to take up space. I'm sure when you were a little kid, you were asked this question a hundred times: "What do you want to be when you grow up?" Try to remember the first answer that popped into your head. Think back, was it a doctor, a lawyer, or an astronaut? What you said back then doesn't matter, but learning to dream again does.

If you could snap your fingers and be anything you wanted to be, do, or have, what would that be?

Remember, desire comes from Spirit. It's given to us for a reason. Listen to your heart, not your head. It's truly frustrating, and painful, to live an inauthentic life, that's why it's imperative to know yourself and your desires.

Clues

What you want and what you need are two different things. NEED, is when you need to buy food to eat. WANT, is what you desire. How do you find out what your WANTS are? Just ask yourself, what do you love to do? What would you do even if you weren't paid to do it?

Are you creative? Do you like to help people? Do you like to cook, teach, sew, or draw? If you still come up empty, go into a bookstore and browse the magazine section. Peruse the travel section, the home section, anything that catches your eye, including the beauty, baby, and children's section. Let your desire guide you, until you hit on something that excites you, and makes you feel like a kid again.

Attend seminars on subjects you might be interested in learning. Check out blogs on the Internet that speak to you. Search for a group or organization you can identify with, and join it.

Never let negative thoughts or doubts invade your space. Do not question yourself about searching for your purpose. Instead, compliment yourself on moving forward towards fulfilling your destiny.

It may seem impossible at first. That's okay. You have to start somewhere. That somewhere has to be a dream. Once you have found what excites you, it's time to build on it.

DO NOT PROCRASTINATE! Take ACTION! Be aware that as soon as you take the first step, you will have negative thoughts. Your mind will flood you with thoughts, such as:

I have to work.
I have no time for dreams.
I have a family to support, dinner to get on the table.

The list goes on and on. You MUST push these thoughts out of your mind. Replace them with:

I can do all things through Christ who strengths me.
I trust that Divine wisdom will guide me.
I can do anything I want, if I put my mind to it.
I will live my dream and make a living doing it.

Remember, negative thoughts are part of the growth process. It's FEAR trying to talk you out of moving forward. When that happens, ask yourself these questions:

If I don't follow my dream, will I become resentful?

How will I know the impact I could have on the world, if I never take a chance?

Will I allow fear to keep me from experiencing the exhilaration of success?

Will I spend the rest of my days thinking "what if?"

If not now, then when?

How will I feel if I miss out on all the happiness, and joy, living my dream could bring to me and my family?

When I come to the end of my life, will I have nothing but regrets?

The time is now! There is always a way to accomplish what you want. You can still keep your day job and begin taking steps towards your dream.

Start with creating a vision board. I know you've heard it a thousand times before, but it works. Place ideas, pictures, and positive affirmations on your refrigerator. Everything starts with a vision. See it, believe it, do it!

Research your ideas or vision. Take a night or weekend class, or an online course. Find a mentor. Volunteer! Follow people on social media who do what you dream about doing. Pray. Have faith. And little by little, your dream will come to pass.

The key to success is a happy heart. Once you are living an authentic life, the rest will follow. Life is a gift! Each day you wake up you have another chance to get it right. Take it! Run with it!

Visualization for Success

(Record this message, so you can listen to it each day).

Set the stage for your visualization. Start by putting on music that you love. Something uplifting, nothing too stimulating, but something that excites you. Light a candle that smells like coffee, or brew a pot. This aroma will lift your spirits and activate your brain cells.

Now, close you eyes. Breathe. Take a few minutes to slow down and de-stress. Visualize a door surrounded by a white light.

See yourself dressed for the occasion. For example, if your dream is to be a chef, see yourself dressed as one.

Next, see yourself walking towards the door and opening it. As you open the door, visualize what's behind it. Again, if you dream of becoming a chef, picture yourself in a bustling kitchen, complete with an entire staff at your disposal.

If your dream is to be an actor, visualize yourself on stage, or in front of a camera, doing a scene. See yourself on the red carpet looking magnificent. Again, picture every detail, down to the jewelry you have on.

The trick to visualization is to be as detail-orientated as possible.

If you desire to have a child, picture yourself pregnant. See yourself holding a baby, nursing it, then picture the room, toys, and crib. See the baby with its tiny features. Touch the child, caress (him or her.) See the image of Jesus standing behind you, see His Light shining down upon you. If you can't picture Jesus, picture Spirit in the form of a Dove sitting on your shoulder. See it. Feel it. Believe it!

After each scenario, see yourself smiling, laughing, happy. Feel the joy, as you slowly open your eyes. Give thanks.

Simple Prayer: Heavenly Father, I wish to serve You. Thank You for helping me to fulfill the dream, and desires, You have placed in my heart.

Note: Ask and it shall be given to you! Believe that it will be!

17

The Challenge

I'D LIKE TO offer you a challenge. A challenge to put aside your judgment, skepticism, and pre-conceived ideas about the subject I'm about to discuss, and come with me into uncharted territory. I promise you won't be disappointed.

Let's suppose you saw someone distributing flyers saying that God is in town, and He's open for business. What would you do? Would you ignore it? I guarantee you would do everything in your power to get to Him. You would stand in line for days just to get a glimpse of Him. People would come from all over the world, and pandemonium would break out, the press and social media would have a field day. Here's where the challenge comes in...

※　※　※

...I'd like you to step out in faith, and call a Catholic Church and ask when they are having adoration. Then go and make a visit.

Wait! Before you leave the page, hear me out. I want you to think about something. Why is it easier for people to believe in the spirit world, tarot cards, reincarnation, and people who claim to talk to your deceased loved one, yet find it impossible to believe that Jesus transformed Himself through the power of the Holy Spirit into a tiny piece of bread? Yes indeed, that little white wafer is the body, blood, soul, and divinity of the crucified Christ. It is not a symbol.

Jesus Himself said, "I am the Bread of Life." He also said He would never leave us. When I watch people line up to receive the Sacred Host at Mass, I realize I'm watching God's word in action. As He gives Himself to us, He fulfills His promise to never leave us in the humblest of ways.

Matthew 28: 20
"And surely I am with you always, to the very end of the age."

I encourage you to take the challenge I set before you, and go to adoration and sit before the Blessed Sacrament. What do you have to lose? Ask Jesus to reveal Himself to you. He will. You will be amazed at the blessings and miracles that will pour down from Heaven upon you. Don't miss the opportunity to meet Jesus up close and personal. I promise it will be something you will never forget.

❋ ❋ ❋

I have a strange story I'd like to share with you. It was a chilly morning in April, I was happy and comfy under my down quilted comforter, when Spirit awoke me. I jumped up, feeling an urgency to get to the chapel. I threw on my coat over my pajamas and ran out of the house. It was 4:30 in the morning and still dark outside.

Upon arriving at the chapel at Saint Paul's, I noticed it was dark inside. At first, I thought it was closed. On second thought, I knew the chapel had to be open 24/7 so I ventured out to see what was going on. I walked up the few steps to the door, and rang the bell. No one buzzed back. Then I turned the knob. To my astonishment, the door opened.

I went inside. It was dark. Jesus was alone. There was no guardian. I was shocked and delighted at the same time. I had a golden opportunity to be alone with Jesus, if only for a little while. Now, I understood why Spirit had woken me. After I had basked in His love, the door opened, and in walked the next guardian. I said a prayer and left. This was a great gift from Spirit, but He wasn't finished with me yet. I figured while I was out, I might as well attend Mass. I had no idea what day it was. I only knew I wanted to go to church. When I walked in the door still in my Pajamas, I was overjoyed to discover it was the feast day of my beloved Saint Anthony. I received two great surprises and blessings that day, simply by following Spirit's call.

If things like that can happen to me, they can happen to you, too! There's nothing special about me. I consider myself nothing more than a sinner.

No matter how you may feel about yourself, never use it as an excuse not to visit Jesus. Often, I have gone before Him, in a sad or depressed mood, sometimes angry, and annoyed. I go to Him anyway. After sitting there for a while, I begin to tell Him how I feel. "I really don't want to be here. I'm in a bad mood. I feel annoyed at everyone, even You." Minutes later, sometimes seconds, I'm joyful and grateful. Sometimes I cry. I can literally feel the transformation taking place. It's amazing how I can go in angry, and come out feeling safe, happy, and secure. It happens every time. If I don't sense the connection, I tell Him, "Lord, I don't feel anything today. I don't know what You want with me? I'm tired and hate to come here and not feel the connection." The next morning I'm a different person. I'm happy, joyful, and giving praise. He never fails.

My intention is not to change who you are, or what you believe. My deepest desire is for you to experience the miracle for yourself.

Simple Prayer: Father my deepest desire is to know You. Reveal Yourself to me.

Note: Ask and you shall receive...

❋ ❋ ❋

Things to Investigate

Padre Pio: Padre Pio (who I found out about ten years ago) is a modern day mystic. He was canonized a Saint by Pope John Paul II on June 16, 2002.

What made him special, was the fact that he lived with the stigmata (the wounds of Christ) for most of his adult life. He suffered terribly. If you want to be mesmerized, research his story. It is truly an eye-opener.

You can also go on YouTube for clips of him with the stigmata. He was an amazing man, and now a great Saint, who answers prayers and performs miracles from the spiritual realm.

He was a mystic in the real sense of the word. He was able to read minds, and appear in two places simultaneously. Lost souls would come to him in the middle of the night, begging him to pray for them.

He had physical battles with the devil. He was once thrown and thrashed across his room, and emerged with battle scars to prove it. He performed many exorcisms while the evil one tormented him.

Pray to him. He is a loving and powerful saint. Upon his death, his wounds healed. He died on Sept. 23, 1968, at 2:30 a.m. in the Monastery of Our Lady of Grace, in San Giovanni Rotondo, Italy. He was 81 years old.

Note

If the information in this book has been helpful to you in any way, or, you have experienced miracles from its teachings, please contact me via email. I would love to hear from you.

Email: ajourneyofmiracles319@gmail.com

Website: Journeyofmiraclesnetwork.com

*Proceeds from this book will help fund future chapels.

Resources

The Bible
Wikipedia
The Shroud of Turin web-site
The Eucharistic Miracle of Lanciano
Eucharistic Miracle in Buenos Aires
Eucharistic Miracles of the World.

Christianitytoday.com (on the Trinity)

Divine Mercy Prayer
EWTN Divine Mercy
Saint Faustina & Saint Faustina's Diary

Our Lady Of Guadalupe
YouTube Our Lady of Guadalupe, findings of Her Garment
Infallible Catholic
Apparitions of The Blessed Virgin Mary

Danny Thomas Story
Saint Jude's Hospital & Danny Thomas
YouTube Norman Cousins
EWTN Padro Pio

CPSIA information can be obtained
at www.ICGtesting.com
Printed in the USA
BVHW041822120619
550856BV00012B/142/P